THE
COMPLETE GUIDE TO
Mental Health

The comprehensive guide to choosing therapy, counselling and psychiatric care

Elaine Farrell

VERMILION
LONDON

To John *'I cannot give the reasons*
I only sing the tunes
The sadness of the seasons
The madness of the moons'
MERVYN PEAKE

First published in Great Britain in 1991 by Macdonald Optima

3 5 7 9 10 8 6 4 2

Copyright © Elaine Farrell

This edition published in the United Kingdom in 1997 by Vermilion, an imprint of Ebury Press
 Random House Group
 Random House
 20 Vauxhall Bridge Road
 London SW1V 2SA

 Random House Australia (Pty) Ltd
 20 Alfred Street
 Milsons Point
 Sydney
 New South Wales 2016 Australia

 Random House New Zealand Limited
 18 Poland Road, Glenfield
 Auckland 10, New Zealand

 Random House South Africa (Pty) Ltd
 Endulini, 5A Jubilee Road
 Parktown 2193, South Africa

 The Random House Group Limited Reg No 954009

 www.randomhouse.co.uk

A CIP catalogue record for this book is available from the British Library

ISBN: 0 09 181520 7

Typeset in Palatino by Deltatype Ltd, Birkenhead, Merseyside
Printed and bound in Great Britain by Mackays of Chatham, plc

Papers used by Vermilion are natural, recyclable products made from wood grown in sustainable forests.

Elaine Farrell is a freelance researcher and writer with an NHS background. She has worked alongside NHS mental health services. She is the author of *Choices in Health Care* (Optima 1989). *Mind – The Complete Guide to Mental Health* is an updated edition of her second book which was entitled *Mental Health: A Survival Guide*.

Books are to be returned on or before the last date below.

02 J 03 **24. JAN 06**

30. J 03

06. OCT   **21. JUN 07**

27 OCT

17. N   **15.** FEB 08

     22|5|15

12 MAR 04 5 |6||5

14 J 04   30|9|21

06. JAN 05

LIBREX –

CONTENTS

Introduction   1

Chapter 1 Mad, bad or just plain sad?   3
How mental distress is classified   4
Neurosis   5
Psychosis   5
Personality disorder   6
Possible causes of mental distress   6
Categories of mental distress   7
Agoraphobia and other phobias   7
Alcohol dependence   10
Alzheimer's disease   12
Anorexia nervosa   12
Anxiety   13
Bereavement   15
Bulimia nervosa   17
Dementia   17
Depression   19
Huntington's chorea   22
Mania   22
Manic depression   23
Obsessive disorders   24
Paranoia   25
Phobias   26
Post-natal depression   26
Post-traumatic stress disorder   29
Seasonal affective disorder   30
Self-harm   31
Sociopathic (psychopathic) disorder   34
Schizophrenia   35

Chapter 2 You know what your problem is,
                 don't you!   39
Understanding stress   41
Stress and you   42
Signs of stress   43
Causes of stress   44
Recognised stress factors   46

Dealing with stress 48
Learning to relax 48
Breathing to relax 48
Relaxation exercises 49
Deep muscle relaxation 50
Self-hypnosis 52
Massage 52
Meditation 53
Yoga 53
Eleven ways to deal with tension 54

Chapter 3 Healthy bodies, healthy minds 56
Alcohol 56
Knowing how much you drink 57
How much should you drink? 59
Diet 59
A healthy diet 60
Exercise 61
Safety 62
Suitability and satisfaction 62
Suppleness, stamina and strength 63
Motivation 63
Getting a good night's sleep 64
Staying well 65

Chapter 4 Growing good? A guide to therapy 66
Choosing therapy 67
Psychotherapy and counselling 67
Analytic psychotherapies 68
  Psychoanalysis 68
  Psychoanalytic psychotherapy 70
  Neo-Freudian analysis 71
  Jungian psychotherapy 71
Post-analytic one-to-one therapies 71
  Gestalt therapy 71
  Primal therapy 72
  Rogerian therapy 72
  Biofunctional therapy 73
  Hypnotherapy 73
Behaviour and cognitive behaviour therapies 73
Group therapy 76

    Family therapy   78
    Marital therapy   79
    Sex therapy and psycho-sexual counselling   79
    Self-help groups   79
  Choosing a therapist   80
    Checking a therapist's credentials   80
    How to judge whether therapy is working   82
    What to do if you feel abused   82
  Availability of therapy   83

Chapter 5 Surviving Community Care   85
  Finding support   87
  Accommodation   88
  Employment   91
  Getting to know people   92
  Helplines   94
  Health care services   94
    Acute hospital care   94
    Day hospitals   96
    Mental health centres   96
  Mental health care professionals   96
  Patient involvement in care regimes   98
  Mental health care services   99

Chapter 6 Mental Health and Human Rights   103
  The Patients' Charter   104
  Human rights   105
  The Mental Health Act 1983   107
    Legal rights under the Mental Health Act 1983   107
  The mental health consumer movement   119
  Patients' councils   119
  **The role of advocacy in achieving mental
    health rights**   120
    Patient or citizen advocacy   120
    Paid advocacy   120
    Self-advocacy   120
  The role of professionals   122
  The Mental Health Act Commission   122

Chapter 7 Drug Treatments   123
  The need for drugs   123

Drugs and their side-effects 125
  Lithium treatment and its side-effects 129
Electroplexy (ECT) 130
  Agreeing to ECT 131

Chapter 8 Alternative Treatments 132
  Acupuncture 132
  Aikido 133
  Alexander technique 133
  Anthroposophical medicine 133
  Applied kinesiology 134
  Aromatherapy 134
  Art therapy 134
  Assertiveness training 135
  Autogenic training 135
  Bach flower remedies 135
  Biofeedback 138
  Chiropractic 138
  Colour therapy 138
  Dance therapy 139
  Drama therapy 139
  Dream work 139
  Exercise 140
  Feldenkrais technique 140
  Flotation therapy 140
  Herbalism 141
  Hydrotherapy 142
  Ionisation therapy 142
  Massage 143
  Music therapy 143
  Reflexology 143
  Rolfing 144
  Shiatsu 145
  T'ai chi 145
  Yoga 145

Resources 147

Useful Addresses 154

Index 160

INTRODUCTION

Mental distress is something that happens to someone else. And when it does, someone else deals with it.

Perhaps that is what many of us like to think, but in fact it's a long way from the truth, as the following evidence demonstrates:

- one in four people suffer from mental health problems
- 20,000 people die each year as a result of mental health problems – four times as many as die in road accidents
- mental health problems are as common as heart disorders, three times as common as cancer and 3,000 times more common than AIDS
- an estimated one in ten recently delivered mothers will experience post-natal depression
- one in ten people experience depression at some time in their lives and this is a particularly likely response to a major loss such as bereavement or at times of life change such as adolescence or retirement
- 3.4 per cent of men and 8 per cent of women are affected by phobias, agoraphobia being the most common phobia presented at out-patient clinics
- alcohol and drug misuse account for one in 20 cases of mental health problems recognised by GPs
- the average risk of developing a schizophrenic-type illness is around eight people in 1,000
- one person out of every 200 will develop mania at some time in their lives

In addition to these figures are the people who never come to the attention of mental health services and are therefore not recorded. They try and cope by themselves or with the support of relatives.

All this goes to show that people who do not experience some form of mental distress at some time during their lives are probably fairly unusual and certainly very lucky. The likelihood is that most of us know someone who has suffered from a mental health problem of some kind. Indeed, many of us may have cared for someone or perhaps wished we had known how to care for someone who was experiencing mental distress. Now that the majority of care for people with mental health problems happens outside hospital, if we have not yet been touched by emotional distress and mental pain, it is probably just a matter of time.

This book has been written to help promote our mental health survival by removing some of the fear and ignorance that surrounds mental distress, by promoting the skills needed to deal with some of the factors that contribute to mental distress, including stress and lack of physical well-being, by offering guidance and information to carers of people with mental health problems, by examining various treatments and therapies that are currently used in the care of mental distress, by providing some knowledge and understanding of the different types of mental health services that are available and by promoting the understanding of and fight for the rights of mental health service users. For more information and support contact your local Mind group or Mind*info*Line, which can provide information on mental health services Mon.–Fri. 9.15 a.m.–4.45 p.m.; tel: 0181-522 1728 (Greater London); 0345 660 163 (outside London).

1

Mad, bad or just plain sad?

We all carry within us the seeds of our own mental health problems. Those who suffer severe forms of mental distress are not 'different'. It is only that they have been subjected to an environment that has allowed their seeds to flourish. Harsh, critical, unaffectionate parents, doting, demanding parents, complicated family relationships, poor nutrition, poverty, unemployment, too little success, too much success, unhelpful coping strategies, all these things and more can destroy our mental well-being. And in the same way as a cactus will not flourish in a rain forest nor a rose in the desert, so some people will not flourish in the environments in which they find themselves.

Evidence suggests that given an environment that nurtures the individual as a whole, many of those at risk from severe mental distress may be spared. Making a hard and fast distinction, then, between the mentally 'well' and the mentally 'ill' is artificial, although it has traditionally made the mentally 'well' feel more comfortable as well as providing some form of care for the mentally 'ill'. Mental health problems of any kind can severely affect someone's ability to live a fulfilling life, particularly in a society that values achievement, success, gain, status and wealth. It is perhaps then not surprising that people fear and often wish to hide mental distress, as to exhibit it openly is to risk being devalued by others. Yet we all experience madness at some times during our lives. Too much to drink at a party can make us behave so 'out of character' that we prefer to forget our behaviour, or we blame it on the alcohol, rather than admit to ourselves that it merely removed our normal inhibitions and allowed out something of ourselves that we might ordinarily prefer to keep hidden. Alcohol causes a change in the biochemical balance of our brains and bodies.

Our vision blurs, our speech slurs, we lose co-ordination, our reflexes are retarded, our behaviour is affected. But as long as we are not too embarrassing or start to damage other people or their property, the loss of control through alcohol is accepted, even encouraged by those around us. However, if we lose control and exhibit bizarre behaviour that we do not understand and the causes of which are *not* known, then there is far less tolerance. In such a case we want the authorities to step in. We want 'mad' people locked away. Losing control then, whether it is a spectacular psychosis or a gradually dawning depression is usually seen as undesirable.

For some people the loss of control is very severe and very distressing, to themselves and others. To hear voices saying bad things about you when there is no one around (auditory hallucinations) or to feel that your mind is being controlled is not something that any of us would choose to experience, but for some people it is a reality. We do not really understand why. But then we do not understand how many medications work, but we accept that they do every time we take them for some ailment.

Some people learn to live with their symptoms and with support and/or medication are able to live their lives as they would wish. However, for many others the onset or repeat of their symptoms means that they are less able to cope with many of the demands of everyday life, and the fear and prejudice that surround their mental health problem mean that they lose out on support. Understanding something about the different ways in which mental distress expresses itself can help the sufferer and cut down on a great deal of prejudice.

How mental distress is classified

The main experiences of mental distress are given clinical classifications or labels. This means that doctors and medical academics have worked towards defining mental distress in terms of signs and symptoms. This approach can have mixed blessings. On the one hand it can mean that people suffering from certain distressing experiences can receive help and support. However, it can also mean that some people become labelled, judged and lose their dignity, their social standing and at times, their human rights. Some people find a diagnosis helpful while others find it confusing and constraining.

As clinical diagnoses do exist and are used in the day-to-day care of people with mental health problems, the definitions are included here to aid understanding. However, it is perhaps most important to remember that a person is not their diagnosis. They may be suffering from a mental health problem that could be defined as being 'anxiety based' or 'schizophrenic in nature', but this does not mean they are a 'neurotic' or 'schizophrenic'. Clinical or medical diagnoses fall into three main groups: neuroses, psychoses and personality disorder.

Neurosis

Mental health problems deemed to be neurotic in nature are those characterised by excessive unhappiness, unhealthy levels of anxiety and unhelpful, perhaps even destructive ways of behaving (referred to as 'maladaptive'). There is usually a loss of perspective rather than a loss of contact with reality and people are usually aware that something is wrong.

The main ways in which a neurosis will show itself are through anxiety, depression or obsessive-compulsive behaviour, although this in itself is usually an expression of an unbearably high level of anxiety.

Phobias, psychosomatic or hysterical illnesses (such as hysterical blindness) also fall into this category.

Mental health problems of a neurotic nature are experienced as exaggerations of normal thoughts and reactions.

Psychosis

A psychosis is usually signified by a loss of a shared reality. The person does not know there is anything wrong with them. They may hold fixed false beliefs, thinking themselves very rich, very powerful or even someone else. They may also experience hallucinations or believe their minds are being controlled by others.

It is often the loss of contact with reality plus the distorted perception (e.g. hearing voices, believing the mind to be controlled by others) that is so frightening for most people.

A psychotic episode can be triggered by stressful events or experiences, drugs, alcohol or other toxins in the body, lack of sleep, a metabolic disorder or infection. However, it can often have no known cause and, depending on the nature of the experience, a person might be diagnosed as suffering from schizophrenia, manic depression or depression.

Personality disorder

The term or diagnosis of 'personality disorder' is largely pejorative and unhelpful. It is often used to describe people who have a set of behaviour patterns which are negative and destructive in nature. From a clinical diagnosis point of view there are 11 or more different types of personality 'disorders', the most emotionally-laden one being 'psychopath' or 'socio-path'.

A sociopath or psychopath is a person who does not experience guilt or remorse at their actions that may cause pain to others. Such people are often impervious to punishment and find it hard to learn from experience. It is their character that appears to be damaged or disordered, rather than their thoughts or mood. They have quite often (although not always) experienced a disturbed upbringing.

Possible causes of mental distress

In reality when people experience mental distress to the extent that they need care, it is often very difficult to get at the root of their experience. For some people whose lives are dominated by their mental distress, with multiple hospital admissions over a period of years, it is their experience to receive a variety of 'diagnoses' from a variety of well-meaning clinicians. Anxiety state, depression, personality disorder and schizo-phrenia were amongst a list of diagnoses attributed to one patient I worked with – and that was before she had reached the age of 30. For that particular person, who went on to survive this labelling and live a 'normal' life, the diagnoses gave her nothing, but only left her with a sense of confusion and frustration. Consequently, what may appear to be a clear-cut diagnosis on paper is far more complicated in experience and can at times result in losing sight of the person the diagnosis is attached to.

The causes of mental distress are complex and the most likely explanation is that several factors (biological, psychological and social) combine to cause the problem. Over the years there have been many opinions, some emphasising physical explanations (particularly heredity) and some emphasising the effects of the environment. There is a belief that while most neuroses are mainly determined by the environment (e.g. cultural influences on women), psychotic mental distress arises when an inherited potential is triggered by environmental stresses.

It is often suggested that genetic factors make some people more susceptible to mental health problems. However, it is the susceptibility and not the problems that is passed on. Stress is seen as a crucial factor in the development of mental health problems.

Categories of mental distress

Whatever the advantages and disadvantages of being diagnosed and/or labelled with a mental health problem, the system exists and so there follows a brief explanation of what these categories or 'labels' are, their signs and symptoms, possible causes and likely treatments. Some will be familiar to you. Many have become part of our everyday language. 'I'm depressed' is a popular substitute for 'I'm fed up' or 'I'm unhappy.' 'He's paranoid' or 'She's a hypochondriac' are not uncommon sayings and usually they are seen as being pretty harmless. Some expressions are quite coy. 'I'm bad with my nerves' is far more acceptable to many people than 'I am mentally ill.'

An important point to remember is that these medical or clinical classifications are designed to describe a cluster of symptoms as a form of shorthand for mental health professionals, not to classify the people themselves.

Agoraphobia and other phobias

A phobia is an exaggerated fear. Perhaps the two best-known phobias are claustrophobia (fear of confined spaces) and agoraphobia.

Agoraphobia is usually seen as a fear of open spaces or the fear of going outdoors, perhaps just the opposite of claustrophobia. However, it is slightly more complicated than this. It is perhaps more accurately described as a fear of *public* places, particularly where return to a safe familiar place is difficult and so some enclosed places like a busy shopping arcade could also trigger an attack. The onset of agoraphobia may be experienced as a panic attack in a particular shop or venue. This panic attack is so unpleasant that the sufferer will then try to avoid that particular setting. However, because the fear is, in reality, most probably linked to something other than the setting in which the attack takes place, the avoidance of the setting does not prevent further panic attacks. These continue to be experienced when the sufferer has to go to the corner of the street to post a letter, into the garden to empty rubbish into the dustbin and eventually even when the sufferer tries to leave the house.

Signs and symptoms:
Feelings of fear when leaving the home which may culminate in a panic attack. Sufferers may feel terrified, be unable to think straight, their breathing will be affected as when extremely nervous, they may break out in a cold sweat, experience palpitations and feel that they are at extreme risk from some unknown source.

Possible causes:
The phobia may well be a response to some underlying anxiety that the patient is not aware of.

What might help:
Although behaviour therapy (*see* page 73) has traditionally been seen as being most effective for phobias, counselling or psychotherapy are gaining in popularity and may well be more effective in the long term as they work towards resolving the underlying causes. Behaviour therapy concentrates instead on the symptoms. The effectiveness of the treatments will depend on the individual sufferer.

Self-help programmes are available and more information can be gained about these from the Phobics Society (*see* Useful Addresses, page 154).

There are many phobias, too many to deal with here. However, for interest I have listed just some that may well be experienced, although often not to a degree that affects quality of life:

animals	**zoophobia**
bacteria	**bacteriaphobia** or **microphobia**
bees	**apiphobia** or **mellissophobia**
being afraid	**phobophobia**
being alone	**autophobia** or **monophobia**
being buried alive	**taphophobia**
being stared at	**scopophobia**
birds	**ornithophobia**
blood	**haematophobia**
blushing	**erythrophobia**
cancer	**cancerophobia**
cats	**ailurophobia**
childbirth	**tocophobia**
corpses	**necrophobia**
crowds	**ochlophobia**
darkness	**nyctophobia**
death	**thanatophobia**
dirt	**mysophobia**
disease	**pathophobia**
dogs	**cynophobia**
dreams	**oneirophobia**
enclosed spaces	**claustrophobia**
fire	**pyrophobia**
flying	**aerophobia**
foreigners or strangers	**xenophobia**
heights	**acrophobia**
heart disease	**cardiophobia**
horses	**hippophobia**
illness	**nosophobia**
insanity	**lyssophobia**
insects	**entomophobia**
light	**photophobia**
lightning	**astrapophobia**
marriage	**gamophobia**
pain	**algophobia**
reptiles	**batrachophobia**

ridicule	**katagelophobia**
Satan	**Satanophobia**
sexual intercourse	**coitophobia**
sharp objects	**belenophobia**
sleep	**hypnophobia**
speed	**tachophobia**
spiders	**arachnophobia**
thunder	**keraunophobia**
travel	**hodophobia**
venereal disease	**venerophobia**
water	**hydrophobia**
women	**gynophobia**
worms	**helminthophobia**

Alcohol dependence

Most people would throw up their hands in horror if you suggested to them that they might use and abuse drugs, and yet they would be quite happy to down a few pints, gin and tonics or glasses of wine, often several times a week and with no fear of the consequences – although there may be some short-term repentance during a severe hangover. Within our culture, it is the people who do not drink alcohol who are seen as distinctly odd. These poor souls are generally ridiculed and badgered for making everyone else feel bad in some perverse way (for some reason alcohol consumption as a form of self-harm is more securely carried out in groups).

Our culture is in fact highly tolerant of alcohol abuse – tolerant, that is, until the abuser loses their entertainment value and becomes a nuisance or out of control, in which case the tolerance ends abruptly and sufferers find themselves without jobs, friends or family and often in the hands of the psychiatric or prison services.

Alcohol dependence sneaks up on people because of its innocent image, and yet the psychological and physical damage it can cause can be devastating and permanent. It is not solely caused through consumption of spirits. Any alcoholic beverage can cause dependence, including beer, wine and cider. It is the alcohol that does the damage, not the form it comes in.

Alcohol dependence can cause depression and psychotic episodes, including auditory and visual hallucinations. It can cause extreme feelings of paranoia and even in some cases dementia through damage to the brain. All this is in addition to the physical damage alcohol consumption can cause to the body. And alcohol doesn't discriminate – it takes victims from all walks of life.

Signs and symptoms:
Increased consumption of alcohol of any kind, particularly if associated with the feeling of a need for a drink. Signs and symptoms grow with the level of dependence and may include memory blackouts, mood changes, impaired thinking and concentration, breakdown of relationships and neglect of self. In the long term hallucinations and trembling can occur.

High levels of alcohol consumption causes widespread damage to the body. Burning through the stomach lining, causing ulceration, alcohol inflames the liver to the point where it cannot regenerate itself. Severe liver damage (cirrhosis) is fatal.

Possible causes:
As with many other mental health problems, the causes can be explained as being physical (i.e. some individuals are more prone because of some inborn predisposition), psychological or social (alcoholism is a greater problem within cultures where drinking is culturally reinforced).

Likely treatments:
Depending on the severity of the problem, a person might need detoxification in hospital (i.e. treatment with drugs to neutralise the very distressing symptoms of withdrawal) followed by some form of therapy. There are a number of support groups, of which Alcoholics Anonymous is probably the best known. Others include Alateen (for teenagers who are alcohol dependent) and Al-Anon Family Groups for relatives and friends of people who are alcohol dependent or who may have relationship problems caused through their drinking habits. Alcohol Concern is another national organisation with local branches and ACCEPT is an organisation that offers free therapy services in the London area.

There are private clinics for those that can afford them. To find out about these, contact Alcohol Concern (*see* Useful Addresses).

Alzheimer's disease

See Dementia.

Anorexia nervosa

Anorexia nervosa has been much publicised in recent years. Affecting an estimated 60,000 to 200,000 people, primarily women in their teens and early twenties, this form of mental distress is an expression of deep emotional conflict which results in the individual experiencing a distressed relationship with food. Someone suffering from anorexia will be obsessed with weight loss and although they may be fascinated by food they will go to extreme lengths to avoid eating. Depression, disordered sleep patterns, restlessness and disturbance of bodily functions are some of the effects.

Signs and symptoms:
Marked weight loss, bones showing under the skin, which is dry and papery sometimes with the growth of a fine downy hair on legs, arms and trunk. Blood pressure drops and the person will feel very cold. In women, the main sufferers, the monthly period will stop. They may go to extreme lengths to avoid eating food, including hiding it about their person.

Possible causes:
Anorexia is believed to be a response to underlying anxieties and misery in relation to life issues such as sexual and other relationships, examinations and work pressure. Because self-inflicted starvation prevents the development of womanhood (by reducing libido, stopping periods and producing a child-ish, waif-like figure), sexual issues are often focused upon, although sufferers who have spoken about their anorexia give a fuller picture and talk of their need to take control of their lives in the only way they can. However, it is important to see

this form of distress in the context of a culture that values slimness in women and where women are constantly bombarded with 'ideal' images of themselves. Having said this, it must be acknowledged that an increasing number of men have been reported suffering with anorexia.

Likely treatments:
Anorexia is a difficult condition to help as often the person's will is so strong it is really only their decision to change that makes the difference. Even so, the problems can be so deeply entrenched that even when people suffering from eating distress do wish to change it can still be very hard. Many treatments have been tried (and are still tried) with little or no effect (for example electroplexy and hypnosis). If a person is to recover, it is the underlying problems which have manifested themselves in the symptoms of eating distress which must be tackled. Counselling therapy, holistic therapies, creative therapies etc. can be of help. If the major stimulus for the anorexia is seen to be originating from the family situation then family therapy might be appropriate.

Group and individual psychotherapy may well be offered by mental health professionals within the NHS. Private therapy is offered by Anorexia Anonymous.

Support may be very important as people suffering from anorexia often feel that professional workers and others find it difficult to understand their situation. Anorexic Aid is a network of self-help groups set up and run by people who have experienced and recovered from anorexia or bulimia (*see* below).

Family support can be offered by Anorexic Family Aid in the form of advice and counselling.

It is important to remember that eating distress is a symptom, not the cause.

Anxiety

Anxiety is something we all experience at certain times, such as when we have an interview for a job, have to sit an exam or perhaps speak in public. It is a high state of physical and mental arousal that enables us to cope with a situation we find threatening or particularly stressful. Linked to our survival mechanism (the autonomic nervous system), this physical and mental arousal equips us to fight or run away from a perceived threat – what is known as 'the fight or flight response'. However, for someone suffering from anxiety the symptoms are experienced to an unbearable degree all or most of the time, even when there is no experience of a particularly threatening nature. This results in an inability to relax when awake or to sleep well and creates an almost intolerable level of mental and physical agitation.

Signs and symptoms:
Tension causing aches and pains, dry mouth, sweaty hands, diarrhoea, pounding heart, mind in turmoil worrying about things out of proportion, difficulty in getting to sleep, agitation, wringing of hands, constantly talking about matters that are causing concern. There may well be a fixation with possible accidents, becoming ill or failure. Acute anxiety may be experienced as a panic attack.

Possible causes:
Anxiety often accompanies or underlies mental distress of various natures.

It is usually caused by unresolved tensions. Explanations as to how these tensions arise vary depending on different schools of thought. However, as with any other form of mental health problem, each individual's experience will be unique.

What might help:
Extreme anxiety may need some form of drug treatment but this is in no way a solution. Counselling or psychotherapy which helps understanding of the causes of the anxiety and works towards resolving underlying conflicts may help an individual develop ways of dealing with their experience. Some forms of therapy can help with symptom control.

Learning relaxation skills may help sufferers deal with their unpleasant symptoms or prevent panic attacks.

Hypnotherapy is an approach that both induces deep relaxation and helps a person to explore the underlying cause of the anxiety.

All these approaches to anxiety management are available on the NHS and access to them should be discussed with a GP. They are also offered by private counsellors and therapists.

Alternative therapies such as acupuncture, homoeopathy and herbalism have been perceived as beneficial by some sufferers of severe anxiety (*see* Chapter 8).

Drug therapies of a tranquillising nature are now avoided wherever possible because although they lessen the symptoms of anxiety, in the longer term they cause their own problems, including addiction. In some cases, anti-depressants are prescribed for anxiety. However, although these lessen the symptoms they do not deal with the underlying problem and again, can have unwelcome side-effects.

Bereavement

Loss is a highly significant contributor to mental distress. People who have suffered significant losses when young are believed to be more vulnerable to depressive episodes and the loss of a loved one is a major life trauma that is most likely to contribute to depression. Indeed, depression is seen as part of the grieving process, as the bereaved person has to accept the loss before they can move on.

Individual people react differently to someone dying. Perhaps you can remember a time when you lost someone. It may be that your own reactions to the death were different from those of another person. Some people appear untouched or unemotional. They do not cry. They seem to get on with their lives very quickly. Others appear very angry or cry all the time. Some people may throw themselves into work whilst others have no energy or motivation.

Although the grieving process is generally accepted as taking about two years to work through, this is not the same for all people and some find it takes longer to move on or for the grief to lessen. There will be times when the sadness and grief feel worse, often around significant dates like anniversaries, birthdays and Christmas. The anniversary of the death is a significant landmark that, whilst bringing feelings of sadness, can also provide a milestone to progress, as each year the sadness lessens and you are no longer so held to the past.

Signs and symptoms:
It is important to remember that bereavement is a normal process. However it is possible for people to get 'stuck' at some stage and need help to move on. The commonly recognised stages of bereavement after a significant loss are:

shock, numbness
denial (an experience of genuine disbelief that the person is dead)
guilt
anger
depression
reconciliation

What might help:
Grieving following a significant bereavement is a painful process that cannot be rushed and, for most people, has to be experienced. Many people are able to get through the aftermath of the loss with the support of friends and family and by working through their feelings themselves. However, there are as many others who feel the need to talk with someone who understands but who is more detached. Special support in the form of counselling is available for such people through organisations such as CRUSE or Compassionate Friends. Your GP may be able to refer you for counselling and in times of crisis, organisations such as the Samaritans can be very supportive.

If the experience of grief is felt as overwhelming anxiety or depression then it may be necessary to have additional help through the use of medication such as an anti-depressant and your GP is the person to speak to about this.

Many people will ask, 'What is the point in having counselling or tablets? It won't bring back the person I love.' That is true. And treatment won't *take away* the suffering. However, it is important not to underestimate how the suffering can be eased as well as experienced when shared with another understanding and empathic person, and how longer-term problems might be avoided by the right type of help from your doctor, support group, counsellor, etc.

Nothing can be done to bring back the person who is lost, but a lot can be done for those left behind.

Bulimia nervosa

Bulimia is a form of eating distress that is characterised by a cycle of eating which may range from total starvation to bingeing on food totalling thousands of calories and then vomiting. As with anorexia (*see* above), the abuse of laxatives and diuretics to purge the body of its waste products may be present. Unlike people with anorexia, however, the sufferers may be any weight or size and may not necessarily look ill.

Signs and symptoms:
Similar to those experienced by someone with anorexia except that people suffering from bulimia tend to have greater insight into what is happening to them. 'Bingeing' may often take place when others are not around. Sufferers may experience tooth decay and gastric erosion from constant vomiting.

Possible causes:
As for anorexia.

Likely treatments:
As for anorexia.

Dementia

There are several different types of illness grouped under the term 'dementia', all of which are characterised by physical changes in the brain, that is, damage caused by disease. These include Alzheimer's disease, Huntington's chorea, Pick's disease and Jakob Creutzfeld's disease.

This damage is progressive and irreversible. The relentless destruction of brain cells leads to a loss of memory and confusion as well as personality and behaviour changes. However, there are a number of other forms of mental distress that can mimic these symptoms, not least depression and toxic confusional states. These can be treated. In some cases brain deterioration due to dementia as well as depression can be present, particularly when the sufferer is aware of their failing abilities.

The terms 'dementing' or 'senile' are increasingly being regarded as derogatory with the accompanying risk that sufferers are consigned to a 'no hope' category of care. With skilful assessment, treatment and care, an individual with dementia's potential can be maximised, as can their quality of life. This in turn can lessen the distress caused to relatives and other loved ones who must watch the irreversible deterioration.

Signs and symptoms:
Marked memory and skill loss are the main signs of dementia or brain deterioration. There may also be a change in personality so that some of their qualities become lost while others become exaggerated. During the early stage of the onset of dementia, there is often a realisation of what is happening and this can in turn lead to other mental health problems such as depression. Anxiety and paranoia can also be experienced.

This type of mental health problem is extremely distressing for the sufferer and relatives and friends. There is no cure for brain deterioration and so it is essential that sufferers' dignity and well-being are maintained with the help of professional and non-professional carers.

Possible causes:
With Alzheimer's disease the brain experiences a physical change. Nerve endings deteriorate and there is a loss of neurotransmitters or 'chemical messengers'. There appears to be some link between the absorption of aluminium into the body's system and brain deterioration.

With other types of dementia damage is caused by restricted blood flow, causing brain cells to die. Strokes are one cause of brain deterioration.

What might help:
Brain deterioration of the kind found in dementia is irreversible and so the emphasis has to be on quality of life. Physiotherapy, reminiscence therapy (short-term memory deteriorates before long-term memory), reality orientation, occupational therapy and speech therapy are all important for a person who is suffering from any form of dementia.

Signs and symptoms:
Someone who is depressed will experience a number of symptoms: they may feel very guilty over minor matters, they may feel miserable, hopeless and despairing. They may feel that they have failed in the past, whether or not this is a realistic perception. Outward signs will include slowness of pace when walking, a tendency to want to stay in bed, lowered head and drooping shoulders. A depressed person may want to avoid others, even close friends and relatives. Their appetite will diminish and they will eat less.

What might help:
The first point to make here is that mild to moderate cases of depression are relatively common, are usually short lived and can clear up by themselves. Unhappiness is not fun, but in many circumstances it is perfectly normal.

However, for some people, depression can become a very serious pervasive condition. If the depression is caught in time, psychotherapy (*see* Chapter 6), exercise, diet, emotional support and understanding can get a sufferer through. In many cases, the person experiencing depression will have enough insight and motivation and hopefully support to work towards getting over their depression, although at times it might feel overwhelmingly difficult.

In the short term, anti-depressants can be prescribed by a GP, but it cannot be over-emphasised that these are only effective for a very short period of time. They can take between two and four weeks to begin to affect the depression and it should be remembered that they only deal with the symptoms of depression and not the underlying causes. These need to be tackled through other means, such as therapy or by a change of lifestyle or situation. If no positive benefits have been experienced, or indeed, if there is a worsening of symptoms, then it is essential to discuss this with the prescriber of the drugs, as many different types of anti-depressants are available. (*See* Chapter 7, with particular reference to wanted and unwanted effects.)

It must be acknowledged that some people find it impossible to deal with their depression without fairly high levels of support, perhaps even needing hospitalisation. This should be recognised as acceptable, rather than a sign of weakness, madness or failure. Where a patient is hospitalised with depression, the likelihood is that drug treatment will be part of a wider regime that includes supportive counselling, occupational therapy (*see* Chapter 7) and close observation from a skilled nursing team. For people whose depression is very resistant, very deep and life-threatening, electro-convulsive therapy (ECT) may be an option. ECT remains a controversial medical intervention for depression and is discussed more fully in Chapter 7.

Depression is often not easy to shift. If you feel that you cannot deal with your depression by yourself, particularly if it is affecting your life in such an adverse way that the consequences (such as the loss of your job) may be devastating and very detrimental, then don't be afraid to ask for help. Asking for help is a sign of strength, not weakness. Your GP may well be able to offer you counselling personally or may refer you on to a specialist such as a community mental health (psychiatric) nurse, counsellor or a clinical psychologist.

If your GP is not helpful, contact your local Mind group or Community Health Council for advice. Their telephone numbers can be found in your local telephone directory.

For people who have found themselves dependent on tranquillisers, or who have been using tranquillisers for a long period of time (from several months to years) and feel they need help and advice to come off them, the National Tranquilliser Advisory Council – Tranx – can provide advice and counselling.

Huntington's chorea

See Dementia.

Mania

This mood disorder is the opposite in nature to depression. Rather than suffering from an absence of energy, extreme unhappiness and despair, people who have a manic episode experience boundless energy, a feeling of euphoria and the belief that they are very successful. Unlike depression, where the sufferer usually knows that something is wrong, the person suffering from mania is unlikely to have insight into their condition. If left untreated, mania can cause a person to collapse and even die from exhaustion.

If the person suffering from mania also experiences, at times, depression, they are said to be susceptible to manic depression (*see below*).

Unlike depression, which is usually a neurotic disorder, mania and manic depression are psychotic disorders.

Signs and symptoms:
Very elated mood, optimistic, excitable and impulsive, masses of energy, often not needing to eat or sleep, can be very disinhibited, particularly sexually, speech can be very fast, with rapidly changing thoughts and ideas. These ideas may often be very grand in nature, the person believing they are very rich or powerful. They will be unaware that anything is wrong with them. On the contrary, they will feel extremely well because they are so 'high'.

Possible causes:
Chemical imbalance in the body or brain, extreme stress, reaction to some drug treatments such as anti-depressants, unconscious reaction against underlying depression.

What might help:
Drug treatment is often necessary in order to slow down and stabilise the person suffering from mania. For extreme cases, major tranquillising drugs such as Chlorpromazine or Haloperidol might be used. In less severe cases it might be possible to stabilise the sufferer's mood with lithium carbonate (*see* Chapter 7). Prevention, particularly in the form of stress management, is essential for people who experience bouts of mania or a manic-depressive condition in order to prevent relapses, which may be stress-induced even with maintenance on lithium.

Manic depression

Depression, as explained in some detail above, is the most common manifestation of mental distress and is something that most people experience to some degree while for some it can be quite severe. For about 5–15 per cent of those suffering from depression their depressive experience alternates with one of mania (*see above*).

Signs and symptoms:
Mania and depression are both described above. The evidence that a person may be suffering from manic depression results from swings from mania to depression, or vice versa, on a cyclical basis. The period between these swings can vary from a few weeks to years.

Possible causes:
Like so many other mental health problems, the contributing factors will include personality type, upbringing, stressors and the ability to cope with them as well as a possible genetic predisposition. Triggers can include relationship difficulties, work pressure or drug abuse.

Likely treatments:
Treatment depends on whether the sufferer is in the depressive or manic phase of their condition. It may be that a person may need to be maintained on lithium (*see* Chapter 7). Psychotherapy as part of a programme of prevention has also been found to be useful. A stress-management programme, wholefood diet (to prevent constipation, particularly if taking lithium), avoidance of alcohol and cigarettes and a measured amount of exercise will all help to maintain a sufferer's well-being. For more information contact the Manic Depression Fellowship, a self-help organisation for sufferers, their relatives and friends (*see* Useful Addresses).

Obsessive disorders

The main obsessive disorder, although it is relatively rare, is known as 'obsessive-compulsive neurosis'. This type of mental health problem expresses itself through a persistent desire to carry out repetitive actions (compulsion) in response to thoughts that constantly occupy the conscious mind (obsession). For example, a person may become preoccupied by the thought that they have not locked the doors and windows to their house. This thought may become so persistent that the person may feel the need to check all the doors and windows.

Although we all experience these types of thoughts and behaviour at some time, they are usually appropriate to something that is going on in our lives, such as checking and rechecking that the alarm clock is set because we are afraid we might oversleep and miss an important engagement. However, when this type of thought/behaviour pattern gets out of hand it becomes a real mental health problem, as it can totally disrupt the ability to live anything like a balanced existence. Checking rituals can take hours. Constant hand washing in response to a wholly exaggerated fear of germs can result in torn, bleeding skin. Although this type of mental health problem may be very difficult to understand, it is certain that it causes a great deal of distress to the sufferer.

Signs and symptoms:
Fear of contamination, intrusive repetitive thoughts, compulsive checking or cleaning, repetitive need to complete rituals or do things in a specific order, fear that something terrible will happen if rituals are not completed.

Possible causes:
Anxiety is a major feature of obsessive-compulsive disorders although it is often impossible to get to what is causing the anxiety, let alone understand why it expresses itself through the performance of rituals rather than, say, agoraphobia. There is a personality type that is referred to as 'obsessive' which is characterised by extreme tidiness and cleanliness. However, there is no proven link between this type of personality and mental health problems of an obsessive-compulsive nature.

Likely treatments:
Behaviour therapy, psychotherapy, relaxation training, drug treatment or ECT (where underlying depression is suspected), family therapy and in very extreme or intolerable cases, psychosurgery. Mind opposes the use of ECT and psychosurgery in the treatment of such disorders.

Paranoia

We have probably all experienced feelings of mild paranoia.

You may have walked into a room, for instance, only to find everybody stopped talking as you appeared. Were they talking about you? Of course, they may have been. But at the same time they may have been talking about something private that they did not want you to hear or it may simply have been a spontaneous lull in conversation. Whatever the reason, you will probably soon forget about it and life will carry on as normal. However, paranoid feelings can sometimes get out of hand, so that any action or innocent comment can be interpreted as a threat or someone 'having a go' at you. Where this is extreme it can become a mental health problem referred to as a 'paranoid disorder'.

Paranoia can also be a feature of a mental health problem of a schizophrenic nature.

Signs and symptoms:
Paranoia usually exhibits itself through exaggerated feelings of suspiciousness, with beliefs about other people who are plotting or conspiring to do someone harm. Sufferers feel watched or persecuted most of the time.

Possible causes:
A paranoid disorder might be triggered by the introduction of a drug into the person's system. This might be an illicit drug such as cannabis or LSD, but equally might be a prescribed medicine that causes an adverse reaction.

Likely treatments:
Medication may well be the first and foremost treatment. However, psychotherapy, a change in living conditions and community support may well help to prevent further attacks.

Phobias

See Agoraphobia and other phobias.

Post-natal depression

The birth of a baby is generally perceived as being a happy event, enthusiastically awaited and celebrated by friends and family alike. However, childbirth and the demands of motherhood can have unexpected consequences for many women and one of these can be post-natal depression.

Post-natal depression can be experienced in one of three forms:

1. *The baby blues*
This is the mildest form of post-natal depression, and is characterised by a tendency to burst into tears for no apparent reason or for reasons that seem trivial. This tearfulness tends to come on 2–4 days after the birth of the baby and is so common that it is perceived as being quite a normal response by most health professionals. However, the 'baby blues' should not be dismissed, as the feelings are often very distressing for the mother and perhaps not understood by those close to her.

2. *Depression*
Affecting one mother in six (and possibly more), this form of depression can come on any time in the first year of the baby's life, but most usually starts when the baby is between four and six months old. It has the usual symptoms of depression and can be mild, moderate or severe.

3. *Puerperal psychosis*
This is the rarest but most severe form of post-natal depression, affecting around one new mother in every 500. It generally starts a few weeks after the birth, with the mother becoming increasingly restless and unable to sleep. She may start to have strange beliefs, such as that the baby has been fathered by the devil or possessed by aliens. She may see, hear or smell things that cannot be experienced by anyone else. She may have powerful mood swings, from high to low and back again. Her behaviour may become increasingly bizarre and difficult to understand.

Signs and symptoms:
- hopelessness
- feeling inadequate
- excessive and perhaps irrational feelings of guilt

- loss of appetite
- tearfulness
- irritability
- poor sleep, including difficulty getting to sleep and early morning waking
- hostility or inability to have loving feelings towards a normally loved partner
- lack of energy and motivation
- poor concentration
- excessive anxiety about the baby's safety and well-being

Possible causes:
The life change brought about by a first baby can be stressful – the loss of the freedom to come and go as one pleases, the isolation this can often bring, the feelings of helplessness brought about while learning to care for a new baby, the difficulties that may be experienced in bonding with the infant. For women who already have a family, the effects a new baby can have on brothers and sisters, particularly as the mother's attention is refocused, can cause stresses and difficulties. As many women reading this will know, having one child can be stressful but usually manageable, having two can sometimes feel like ten.

Any other stressors that the mother is experiencing, such as a bereavement, house move, poverty or illness, can increase the possibility of post-natal depression occurring. A woman is also more vulnerable if she has three or more children under the age of 14 and has no support or someone to talk to.

Sometimes the unresolved grief of earlier events in the mother's life can be triggered at or after the birth.

On top of the social and emotional consequences of having a baby, the hormonal changes the mother experiences can also have a marked effect on how she feels. The hormone progesterone is produced by the body in large quantities during pregnancy, but this stops at delivery and does not recommence until a fortnight before the first period, which can be some considerable time after childbirth. Some doctors believe that this hormonal change can trigger post-natal depression.

What can help:
Post-natal depression should not be underestimated. A mother

who is suffering from depression needs help, sometimes from professionals, and she should be encouraged to seek it. Talking to a doctor, midwife, health visitor, community psychiatric nurse, psychiatrist or counsellor may provide valuable support.

There are voluntary organisations who are experienced in helping with post-natal depression, such as MAMA or the National Childbirth Trust.

Wherever possible, avoid becoming isolated. Try to stay in contact with other mothers, perhaps through mother and baby groups. Ask for help from friends and relatives so that you are able to have a break, no matter how short.

Try to ensure that you eat properly and get as much rest as is possible under the circumstances.

Above all, do not be afraid of talking your difficulties through with someone you can trust, or, if necessary, with a professional helper.

Post-traumatic stress disorder

This is the term given to the onset of a range of symptoms following a psychologically distressing event which is outside the usual range of human experience, typically some form of disaster or the witnessing of violent and multiple death, but it can also be the reaction to some form of abuse or torture.

Not everybody experiences PTSD following a traumatic event and there is no time limit on when the symptoms may arise, as this may depend on other triggers. However, a sufferer of PTSD will be recognised by the following emotional and physical reactions:

- recurring thoughts and pictures of the incident
- feelings of intense distress at symbolic reminders of the event
- flashbacks
- nightmares
- excessive activity in order to avoid thinking about the trauma
- avoidance of situations that trigger memories of the trauma
- emotional detachment and numbness, with difficulty in expressing affection

- reluctance to plan for the future
- inability to have refreshing sleep
- irritability and aggression
- poor concentration
- feelings of anxiety or panic

What might help:
It is generally recognised that expressing the distress due to the trauma is important, regardless of whether that happens formally or informally, with friends or professional counsellors, immediately after the event or when the need arises. It is believed that 'bottling up' the feelings or dealing with the distress with alcohol or drugs may cause longer-term and perhaps more severe problems.

Professional help is available from a number of sources and your GP will be able to refer you to your local service. The type of help that is available generally comes in the form of behavioural therapy, where a clinician, usually a psychologist or a specially trained nurse, will take the sufferer repeatedly through the trauma in fantasy so that they re-experience the emotions they felt at the time. This may need to happen many times before the emotions are dealt with and the person no longer feels so uncomfortable and anxious.

Cognitive therapy is another approach favoured with PTSD. This works by challenging self-damaging thoughts and beliefs, such as 'It was my fault' or 'I should have done something to stop it', and allows the person to see the traumatic event more realistically.

There are a number of self-help groups, professional organisations and general services that can help with PTSD, and these are listed in the Useful Addresses section.

Seasonal Affective Disorder (SAD)

Seasonal Affective Disorder is believed to affect 1–3 per cent of the population each year between the months of October and April, whilst a further 20 per cent experience something referred to as 'winter blues' or sub-syndromal SAD. This occurs during December, January and February.

The effects of SAD can be quite disabling, causing a decline in day-to-day functioning which needs treatment. It seems to most commonly affect people between the ages of 18 and 30.

Someone who experiences several of the symptoms three or more winters running may well be suffering from Seasonal Affective Disorder.

Signs and symptoms:
- sleep problems, with oversleeping, continual tiredness, disturbed nights or early morning waking
- no energy
- overeating
- feeling sad, hopeless or despairing
- social withdrawal
- anxiety, tension and inability to cope with life's stresses
- loss of interest in sex or physical contact
- mood changes

What might help:
As well as the strategies and treatments for general depression, there are indications that treatment with sun lamps (UV light) can help Seasonal Affective Disorder, although sun beds are increasingly being seen as a possible health risk in relation to skin cancer. Light treatments are available which use screened UV rays which are not harmful. The most usual is the light box. These are available from the SAD Association (*see* Useful Addresses).

Self-harm

To cause harm to oneself or others would generally be agreed to be unacceptable or unwanted. It can sometimes therefore be very difficult to come to terms with self-harming or self-abusive patterns of behaviour, such as taking overdoses or cutting parts of one's body. However, for some people, self-harming is a powerful form of expression, and should not be dismissed as manipulative or attention-seeking, as it is usually a desperate attempt by somebody to communicate something that cannot be recognised or perhaps spoken.

More than this, it is perhaps useful to see such extreme forms of self-harm as just that, an extreme form of self-harm that can include alcohol abuse, cigarette smoking, overworking, not eating properly or other forms of neglecting physical and emotional needs.

Why do people harm themselves?

There appear to be a number of 'driving forces' involved in acts of self-harm. Feelings of anger, aggression, frustration, hurt and destructiveness have been identified by therapists working with people who self-harm, particularly if the individual is detached from those feelings and unable to separate, identify and articulate them in a less harmful way. For many people who self-harm, the force of the mixed-up emotion is so overwhelming that the only way to relieve the tension and distress is to hurt themselves, to experience the pain physically. Self-harm can take place without the desire to die being present, which is why sometimes it is not taken as seriously as it needs to be by some health staff.

Who self-harms?

There are no accurate statistics available about the numbers of people who self-harm, as it is often very difficult for people to talk about. However, women tend to self-harm more than men, and this is believed to be due to the social and cultural pressures on women to take care of the needs of others, often denying their own needs and feelings. Men locked up in institutions who are less able to express their anger and frustration openly are more vulnerable to self-harming behaviour. Young people may also engage in self-harming behaviour through pent-up emotion, but they are also subject to enormous pressures – from school, parents and peers – to be something they may not be comfortable with or ready for. In some circumstances and environments it is also possible for there to be peer pressure to self-harm, for example by cutting initials or names into the forearm.

Experience tends to reveal that many, although not all, self-harmers have been sexually abused at some time in their life.

What might help:

As with many forms of mental distress, having an experienced and skilled counsellor or therapist to talk to can help someone move forward. It is often more helpful to work at understanding the underlying causes of the self-harming than to tackle it directly, although a more behavioural approach, concentrating on finding distractions, other channels for feelings and understanding the triggers to the behaviour, is also used by some therapists. There appear to be few counsellors who specialise in helping self-harmers and the local NHS mental health services may be the best option. Ask your GP for a referral to the local community psychiatric nursing service, as this is likely to be more responsive in terms of time than the clinical psychology service, who generally have a waiting list months long.

There are also specialist organisations, such as the Bristol Crisis Service for Women, or Hidden Scars in Salisbury, which may help. Your local Mind organisation may well be able to put you in touch with these or any other self-help groups.

Self-help:

Some people feel that they can, and would rather, tackle their self-harming behaviour themselves. Some ideas for helping in this case are:

- To make the decision to stop, or to try to stop. This is the first step.
- Do not beat yourself up for self-harming. You are not to blame. Your self-injury is an expression of powerful negative feelings. You are not a bad person.
- Keep notes or a diary of what is happening when you feel the need to harm yourself. This will aid understanding and, over a period of time, will help you devise strategies for coping with the overpowering feelings that contribute to the self-harming.
- Try to find someone, if only one person, whom you can confide in. The Samaritans are there to listen and not judge and may well be useful. It is a confidential service and you do not even need to give your real name.
- Try drawing or painting how you feel. Try painting on yourself in bright colours.
- Write a list of positive things about yourself and keep this somewhere visible. Read it a lot!
- Think about your anger and what you do with it. If you were not being angry with yourself, whom would you be

angry with? Write down what you are angry with them for.
- Kick and hit something that does not cause you injury. Use cushions or soft furniture that will absorb the blows without damaging you. You deserve more than that.
- Try anything that helps!
- If you need to carry out the self-injury, say, by cutting yourself, take care of yourself by ensuring you use clean equipment such as razors. When you feel calmer, cleanse and dress the injury. If it needs medical attention, then get this for yourself, ideally from a sympathetic source, although these are still in short supply.

It is important to remember that for you your self-injury is an important way of dealing with something, regardless of how others may see it. When you decide that you do want it to stop, it needs to be recognised that either something else more positive needs to take its place or that the need to self-injure must go.

Sociopathic (psychopathic) disorder

Although sociopaths, more commonly known as psychopaths, are dealt with by the mental health services and are included in the Mental Health Act 1983, their problem is one of personality as opposed to disorder, although they can, of course, also experience mental health problems such as depression.

The reason for the increasing preference for the term 'sociopath', as opposed to 'psychopath', is the belief that it is external, social, forces that are the main causes of the personality disorder rather than something inherently wrong with the person's psyche.

Signs and symptoms:

A sociopath can be described as someone who persistently commits offences or who behaves aggressively without any experience of conscience, that is, they have no sense of what is right or wrong, good or bad.

Not all people with personality disorders end up in prison hospitals. Much depends on the nature of their offence. However, they will experience and show a total disregard for the feelings or needs of others. It is this lack of feeling, conscience or understanding of right or wrong that can make such a person dangerous.

What might help:
An extensive programme of therapy, treatment to control aggressive symptoms and skilful rehabilitation. Therapeutic communities (*see* Chapter 5) where the social milieu and group work are the main methods of therapy are a progressive approach to this type of problem.

Schizophrenia

Schizophrenia is the best-known 'madness', but one which is hard for most people to understand. Although the word does literally mean 'splitting of the mind', the term 'split personality' is a misnomer.

Some health care professionals will talk of schizophrenia or schizophrenics as if it is a clear-cut illness, with regular symptoms, such as chicken pox. However, in reality it is not that simple. There are symptoms that are generally recognised as being indicative of a schizophrenic illness, although some of them can also be an indication of another psychotic illness, such as manic depression or acute alcohol poisoning. There are also international and transcultural differences when it comes to defining schizophrenia.

Many people who have been on the psychiatric treadmill for a considerable period of time may have been diagnosed in various ways, including as schizophrenic, depending on the diagnosing psychiatrist at the time. Other factors are at work too. If you are black and living in England you are seven times more likely to be diagnosed as schizophrenic than a white person. In the article 'Mental Health and the Black Community', Ade Coker cites the fact that in Barnsley Hall, a large psychiatric hospital in Birmingham, 50 per cent of the patient population are black and that the most common diagnosis for black people suffering from acute stress is schizophrenia. In the United States, people suffering from the same signs and symptoms as a person diagnosed as schizophrenic in England would be diagnosed as manic depressive. In the Soviet Union there was (until glasnost at least) an illness called 'political schizophrenia' (not a literal translation). Political dissidents would be 'offered' asylum in mental institutions as their beliefs were often seen as a sign of their 'illness'.

In a research experiment in the early 1970s, an American psychologist, D. L. Rosenhan, set up an experiment whereby eight people with no experience of a diagnosable form of mental distress gained admission to mental hospitals. They did this by reporting to the admitting officer that they had heard voices saying 'empty', 'hollow' and 'thud'. These words were chosen as they could be interpreted as an hallucinating person feeling that their life was empty and hollow. This could be seen as an existential crisis (a crisis of living) and there had never been a report of an existential psychosis. Once admitted, the 'patient' behaved perfectly normally and stopped simulating symptoms. However, in no instance did the clinical staff realise that the person was not 'mad'. Once in hospital and diagnosed, staff continued to see the person as 'schizophrenic' and to record normal behaviour such as writing notes as evidence of illness.

Signs and symptoms:

● *Passivity experience*
The belief that thoughts are being controlled by others (e.g. aliens) or can be heard by others (thought broadcasting).

● *Auditory hallucinations*
The sufferer hears voices that may well be talking to or about them, usually in a critical or derogatory manner.

● *Primary delusions*
A person may have a complicated false fixed belief, such as that the IRA are out to kill them and that nurses or relatives are members of the IRA.

● *Emotional blunting*
People experiencing this type of mental health problem may be unable to show their emotions or may show emotions that are inappropriate, e.g. laughing at something very sad.

- *Withdrawal*
The person may retreat into a fantasy world where they feel safe.

- *Disorder of expression*
The person may use strange, made up words (neologisms) or words and sentences that do not make sense (e.g. 'owrd salad').

- *Disorder of thought*
The sufferer may experience one or more disorders in the way they think. For instance they may believe that certain things have a special meaning for them (ideas of reference) or find it impossible to think in abstract terms (concrete thinking).

Possible causes:
There is no concrete evidence of the causes of schizophrenia, although there is no doubt that severe stress and life problems can trigger psychotic symptoms in some people; other people have beliefs that to them are very real, although they are beyond the comprehension of others; drug abuse can create schizophrenic-type reactions. Research has shown that it may well be possible to inherit a predisposition to schizophrenia, although this form of mental distress cannot be inherited like eye colour and no 'schizophrenic gene' has been identified. Certain family relationships and ways of communicating are also felt to contribute to the onset of schizophrenia. Whilst sufferers experience changes in the levels of dopamine, a chemical in the brain, it cannot be stated with any degree of certainty that dopamine has a role in causing schizophrenia.

What might help:
About one third of people diagnosed as having schizophrenia only experience one episode, another third have future episodes with periods of remission in between and the remainder experience it as a chronic condition they have to live with for the rest of their lives.

It is widely felt that there is little or no alternative to drugs for people who suffer from a schizophrenic-type condition. However, this depends on the individual and the care available to them.

For some it is believed that psychotherapy is effective (*see* Chapter 4). Certainly some people who have suffered from schizophrenia have found this approach useful, although it seems to be difficult to convince psychiatrists of the possible benefits. Life in an environment that is able to support someone who has had an acute schizophrenic experience and who is vulnerable to relapse because of their home situation may bring benefits.

However, with the current state of knowledge about this disorder it seems that the greatest opportunity, apart from medication, has to lie in the prevention of relapse. Self-care, as described for people suffering from depression (*see* page 19) and described in more detail in Chapter 3, may help a vulnerable person avoid relapse, as may understanding, support and relatively stress-free social conditions.

You know what your problem is, don't you!

Amateur psychologists are as common as cat's fleas. And usually just about as welcome. They lurk everywhere. Often disguised as friends or relatives, they lie in wait until you are feeling either extremely happy or extremely miserable, at which point they look up in front of you, eyes misty with sympathy, head nodding from sheer weight of their burgeoning wisdom and then bestow upon you, lucky soul, the full benefit of their insight. Of course, they say, you know what your problem is! They then proceed to tell you, in your own interests of course, where you don't quite measure up to, well, whatever it is we are all supposed to measure up to. No one's perfect, of course, but really, couldn't you try just a little harder?

You, of course, probably did know what your problem was, but had done a passably good job of denying it. Now, thanks to your benefactor's insight, denial, your number one coping strategy, has taken a mortal blow. If you were feeling happy, sure as eggs are eggs, you don't any more. If you were feeling as miserable as sin and life was looking pretty hopeless in any case, then you might as well make your way to the top of a very tall building or to the bottom of a very deep river.

In most areas of our lives there is always someone or something around to remind us of our shortcomings – advertising, competition, sexual stereotyping, social norms . . . Psychologists establish what is normal and abnormal, average and below average, typical and atypical, and manufacturers, the media, the medical profession, educationalists and a whole score more respond not to uniqueness, individuality or eccentricity, but to that bit of us that can comfortably be counted and categorised. Ideals are held up against which we are measured or against which we should measure ourselves.

The problem with ideals is that they are usually unattainable for all but a few. There can usually only be one winner of a competition or best pupil in a class. Also, they are often artificially created, like advertising images, and change with the times. The one changing ideal that makes me grin through gritted teeth is the cultural swing in bosoms. One year the 'fashion' headlines will pronounce 'Big boobs are in', the next year 'Big boobs are out'. Radical surgery and breast binding aside, it is virtually impossible to successfully manipulate the size, shape or proportion of one's chest in order to maintain social approval. However, for centuries women have tried to do this and corsetry manufacturers have no doubt become very rich on the proceeds.

So much emphasis is placed on how we look rather than what we are that an enormous amount of our very precious time and energy is wasted on pleasing others and losing ourselves in the process. By chasing some elusive illusion of perfection we competently entrench ourselves in no-win situations.

No-win situations by no means just affect women. A man might risk his life in order to conform and yet be rejected because of a change in events outside his control. US soldiers who fought in the Vietnam war found themselves in a no-win situation of horrendous proportions. There were those who seriously doubted the morality of the war (if any war can be called moral), but were nonetheless conscripted. Faced with a conflict between their beliefs and the public view of the war they were required to enter, some registered as conscientious objectors, were called cowards and punished. Others fought because they believed it was the right thing to do, but when the war became unacceptable and was lost, were rejected by American society. The result was that many Vietnam veterans suffered severe psychological hardship both during and after the conflict. And there have been many suicides.

Of course, some people are better at dealing with life crises than others, and it is often how we learn to cope with life's little knocks during our early years that has such an important bearing on how we cope with what become life's body blows later on.

As we grow up, we have to cope with an increasing level of responsibility. We become aware of the expectations others have of us and develop our own expectations. We find ourselves in a world where we have to 'succeed', and where success and achievement have been defined by others. Our parents, peers, employers, patrons, all these and more make it very difficult for us to define for ourselves what we want out of life. Life and our mental health become a matter of knowing ourselves and what we want, achieving what we can and coming to terms with what we can't.

There are different demands on us at different times in our lives, some inevitable, some self-inflicted. Moving house is usually a self-inflicted stress, whereas being made redundant is not. How we cope with these demands is to a large extent how we grow as people. When faced with a demand, we check our resources. Can we cope? If yes, we move ahead, fairly confident of a positive outcome. If we perceive our resources as being inadequate, we may ask for help or develop our resources in some way. However, it is when we feel our resources are inadequate and we are unable to gain further resources that we can start to feel overwhelmed, or in popular terms, stressed.

Understanding stress

Stress is a very individual thing. What one person may find unbearably stressful another might thrive on. For instance, I feel quite ill just watching brokers working in a City stock exchange, waving their arms about with a telephone glued to their ear. To think that some of those people have travelled for over two hours on an overcrowded commuter train makes me want to question their sanity.

The level of stress felt appears to depend on the individual's perception of the stressor as well as their perception of their ability to deal with the situation.

Hans Selye, one of the pioneers of stress research, identified four levels of stress:

Understress: Too little stress takes away the sense of challenge in our lives and with this our feelings of achievement. We are unmotivated and lose our sense of purpose.

Eustress: At this stage we are getting just the right amount of stress in our lives, not too little, not too much. Our lives are fairly well balanced and we feel in control.

Overstress: When we are overstressed we experience a very uncomfortable level of stress. There is never enough time to get everything done. We cannot relax or take time off from work without feeling guilty. However, we find that no matter how hard we work, we never seem to achieve what we set out to.

Distress: Once this stage is reached we are very much out of control. We become ill, either physically or mentally. We may turn to short-term stimulants such as alcohol, sleeping pills or tranquillisers. If unalleviated, this level of distress can kill us.

Stress and you

Understanding ourselves and those things that make us feel stressed is an essential part of a mental health self-care regime. However, before you can cope with stress in a positive and effective manner, you need to become skilled at recognising your own stress responses.

Recognising when we are under stress is not as easy as it sounds. Damaging stress tends to be insidious. It builds up without our noticing over a period of time. Because the mind and body have a tremendous capacity for adaptation, we feel that we are in charge or in control of our responses for quite some time after the damage has begun. It is a little bit like drinking alcohol – by the time we get to the stage where we recognise we have had enough it is often too late and the effects overwhelm us. Stress, like alcohol, distorts our perception.

When we are stressed, we start to notice symptoms like fatigue, waking up feeling tired, lacking motivation to do even fairly simple tasks. If left too long we can get to a stage where we can hardly function, and may collapse, physically or mentally. It is important to realise then that understanding how we respond to various stresses, our strengths and our weaknesses in certain situations, and how we feel as we become stressed, are vital in the prevention of mental health problems and the promotion of general well-being.

Signs of stress

The signs of stress can include:
- marked loss of concentration
- feelings of tiredness, even on waking
- early morning waking
- difficulty getting to sleep
- nightmares
- increased use of alcohol or cigarettes
- increased irritability
- loss of perspective
- tendency to withdraw from social activities
- increased sensitivity to criticism
- change in eating patterns
- tension
- rebelliousness
- stomach pains
- shaky hands
- nervous twitch
- loss of self-confidence
- memory lapses
- uncomfortable feelings of pressure
- palpitations
- stiff jaw
- nail biting
- nausea
- diarrhoea
- panic attacks
- feelings of anger, aggression and hostility
- tearfulness
- neglected appearance
- physical agitation
- dry mouth
- sweaty hands, cold fingers
- grey complexion
- haggard looks

- strong feelings of guilt

Causes of stress

Stress is the result of pressure being applied to one thing by another. Depending on the amount of pressure applied and the object's ability to resist or bend with it, the object will not snap or break. Take, for instance, a strand of uncooked spaghetti. If you take it gently between the fingers of each hand and bend it gently, it will take quite a bit of pressure before it snaps.

Our wrists and ankles are designed to take quite a bit of pressure and bend quite flexibly. However, too much pressure too quickly can result in pain or even a fracture. The same applies to our minds.

Psychologically, we are usually very good at adapting to the level of pressure around us. However, when that pressure gets too great we start to feel psychological pain. And if the pressure is kept up or is forced on us before we are ready to deal with it, our psychological structure can also snap.

How stressful is your lifestyle?

		1 2 3 4 5 6 7	
1.	Doesn't mind leaving things temporarily unfinished	[] [] [] [] [] [] []	Must get things finished once started
2.	Calm and unhurried about appointments	[] [] [] [] [] [] []	Never late for appointments
3.	Not competitive	[] [] [] [] [] [] []	Highly competitive
4.	Listens well, lets others finish speaking	[] [] [] [] [] [] []	Anticipates others in conversation
5.	Never in a hurry when pressured	[] [] [] [] [] [] []	Always in a hurry
6.	Able to wait calmly	[] [] [] [] [] [] []	Uneasy when waiting
7.	Easy-going	[] [] [] [] [] [] []	Always full speed ahead

8. Takes one thing at a time [] [] [] [] [] [] [] Tries to do more than one thing at a time, thinks about what to do next

9. Slow and deliberate in speech [] [] [] [] [] [] [] Vigorous and forceful in speech (uses a lot of gestures)

10. Concerned with satisfying own self, not others [] [] [] [] [] [] [] Wants recognition by others for a job well done

11. Slow doing things [] [] [] [] [] [] [] Fast doing things (eating, walking)

12. Easy-going [] [] [] [] [] [] [] Hard-driving

13. Expresses feelings openly [] [] [] [] [] [] [] Holds feelings in

14. Has a large number of interests [] [] [] [] [] [] [] Has few interests outside work

15. Satisfied with job [] [] [] [] [] [] [] Ambitious, wants quick advancement on job

16. Never sets own deadline [] [] [] [] [] [] [] Often sets own deadline

17. Feels limited responsibility [] [] [] [] [] [] [] Always feels responsible

18. Never judges things in terms of numbers [] [] [] [] [] [] [] Often judges performance in terms of numbers (how much, how many)

19. Casual about work [] [] [] [] [] [] [] Takes work very seriously (works weekends, brings work home)

20. Not very precise   [] [] [] [] [] [] [] Very precise
                                              (careful about
                                              details)

Total score —————————

20–30   Type B2, relaxed and easy-going
30–59   Moderate type B, coping well
60–79   Neither type A nor type B but a healthy AB
80–108   Moderate type A or A2 who should be cautious
109–140 Extreme type A or A1

Recognised stress factors

Major life events are seen as being particularly stressful. These
are listed below.
● divorce
● jail term
● marital separation or equivalent
● death of a close family member
● personal injury or illness
● marriage
● loss of job
● marital reconciliation
● retirement
● change in family member's health
● pregnancy
● sex difficulties
● addition to family
● business readjustment
● change in financial state
● death of a close friend
● change to different line of work
● change in number of arguments with spouse
● taking out a large mortgage or loan
● foreclosing on mortgage or loan
● change in work responsibilities
● son or daughter leaving home
● trouble with in-laws

- outstanding personal achievement
- spouse begins or stops work
- starting or finishing school
- change in living conditions
- revision of personal habits
- trouble with the boss
- change in work hours or conditions
- change in residence
- change in school
- change in recreational habits
- change in church activities
- change in social activities
- taking out a small mortgage or loan
- change in sleeping habits
- change in number of family gatherings
- change in eating habits
- holiday
- Christmas season
- minor violation of the law

Holmes and Rahe
Schedule of Recent Life Events

These are stressful events that happen to most people. By themselves they can cause varying degrees of emotional pain and discomfort, but are usually manageable. What causes difficulties for us is:

- experiencing several of these together
- experiencing a major stressful event in the context of an already stressful context, for example someone who is a single parent may be coping with being without a supportive partner and living on a low income but find it difficult to cope with the additional stress of their mother becoming ill or the death of a close friend. The old saying 'the straw that broke the camel's back' is a useful one to bear in mind.

Sometimes the gradual erosion of our confidence and feelings of self-worth and security, such as through bullying, can also be highly stressful.

Dealing with stress

We all have ways of dealing with stress. Many of them we use unconsciously, partly perhaps because we do not actually consider ourselves 'under stress'. Alcohol is one way in which we 'unwind'. Shouting at family members or kicking the cat are other ways. However, these methods of dealing with stress can have adverse effects – for us, those around us and, of course, the cat.

What we need to cultivate is a range of more positive, healthy methods of dealing with stress, methods that promote our mental well-being rather than threaten it further. Some positive ideas include:

- Walk away from what is causing you the stress (if only to come back and deal with it when you feel stronger).
- Take your mind off the stressor (by absorbing yourself in a hobby, film, book etc.).
- Develop skills to help you deal with the stressor (assertiveness training, simple car maintenance, relaxation techniques or meditation).
- Let off steam in a way which causes no harm (shout, scream, hit a pillow).
- Breathe deeply.
- Have a bath.
- Give yourself a treat.
- Sleep.
- Think of times when you have dealt with stress effectively before.
- Find someone to talk to.
- Share your time with people who are rewarding, not those who are critical and judgemental.
- Join a support group if appropriate.

Learning to relax

Breathing to relax

How we breathe is important to our understanding of, and coping with, tension, anxiety and stress. It affects the levels of oxygen and carbon dioxide in our blood, which in turn affects how well we feel.

Fast breathing mainly from the upper chest is symptomatic of anxiety. Slow breathing, using the lower parts of the lungs with particular emphasis on the out breath, contributes to a lowering in feelings of anxiety. In times of emergency, feelings of anxiety can be lowered by breathing into a paper bag for several minutes or until symptoms subside. This cuts down on the amount of oxygen in the body by breathing in exhaled carbon dioxide.

Although it was once believed that taking deep breaths in front of an open window was the key to well-being, it is now known that it is detrimental to take in too much oxygen. Hyperventilation can be experienced by unfit young people who engage in a sport such as squash or running and who are constantly gasping for air, resulting in dizziness and fainting.

To know if you are breathing correctly, lie on your back, place one hand on the upper part of your chest and the other on top of your tummy. Breathe out first and then breathe in. If you are doing this comfortably, your tummy will rise at the beginning of the breath. If your chest moves first, your breathing is inefficient. After breathing out, wait a moment before breathing in as much air as the body wants. A few breaths like this before starting relaxation will be beneficial. Controlled breathing can be very helpful whenever you are in a stressful situation, such as a job interview or meeting difficult people.

If anxiety and tension make you want to cry in difficult situations (crying releases tension), but it would be better for you to control this, take a deep breath and hold it while pushing the sob down to where you can control it.

Relaxation exercises

Before doing relaxation exercises, it helps to do some gentle stretching exercises. This is because much of the pain and discomfort we experience, such as headaches, neck and shoulder pains, cramps, pains in joints and so on, are created through muscular tension that is stimulated by the mind.

If our mind tells our body that we need to be alert because there is some threat (a deadline not being met, an aggressive boss picking up a mistake we have made, insufficient money to meet our basic needs), the body responds by getting itself into the 'fight or flight' mode. That is, we feel the need to respond to threats by fighting the source or running away. This was particularly important in the days when we were hunters and when the fight or flight mechanism triggered an actual physical response. However, today many threats are psychological and it is much harder to run away from what is in our minds (hence many people's need to use alcohol and drugs). Added to this is a general lack of physical exercise, which means that the products of muscle tension are not burnt up by the body. These waste products build up and make people feel unwell. Muscle relaxation aids their disposal.

Most mental health centres run relaxation groups, as do mental health day hospitals, some GP clinics and evening class groups. It is also possible to purchase relaxation tapes and quite often magazines, particularly for women, include guidance on relaxation.

Deep muscle relaxation

The method of relaxation that has perhaps been most favoured is deep muscle relaxation, because psychologists have discovered that deep muscle relaxation and anxiety cannot exist simultaneously. Therefore, by relaxing you can gain a great deal of control over anxiety, which accompanies many mental health problems, as well as being a problem in its own right.

Everyday stress creates a build-up of stimulation in a certain part of the brain known as the hypothalamus, thereby preventing over-sensitivity to further stress and eventually a form of overload. Deep muscle relaxation is a way of cutting down on the stimulation to the hypothalamus.

Once skilled at deep muscle relaxation you will achieve a greater sense of mental and physical balance and an enhanced sense of well-being. It is, however, a skill that has to be learnt, and like any new skill, this takes time and practice.

Here is one approach to deep muscle relaxation:

Preparation
Sit in a comfortable chair, or better still, lie down. Choose a

quiet, warm room and a time when you are not too tired and will not be interrupted.

If you are sitting, take off your shoes, uncross your legs, and rest your arms along the arms of the chair.

If you are lying down, lie on your back, with your arms at your sides.

Close your eyes, and be aware of your body. Notice how you are breathing, and where the tensions in your body are. Make sure you are comfortable.

Breathing

Start to breathe slowly and deeply, expanding your abdomen as you breathe in, then raising your rib cage to let more air in until your lungs are filled right to the top. Hold your breath for a couple of seconds and then breathe out slowly, allowing your rib cage and stomach to relax, and empty your lungs completely.

Do not force your breathing. After a time, breathing this way will feel natural.

Keep this slow, deep rhythmic breathing going throughout your relaxation session.

Relaxation

Now curl your toes and press your feet down. Tense up on an in breath, hold your breath for ten seconds while you keep your muscles tense, then relax your muscles and breathe out at the same time.

Now press your heels down and bend your feet up. Tense up on an in breath, hold your breath for ten seconds; relax your muscles on an out breath.

Now tense your calf muscles. Tense up on an in breath, hold for ten seconds; relax your muscles on an out breath.

Now tense your thigh muscles, straightening your knees and making your legs stiff. Tense up on an in breath; hold for ten seconds; relax your muscles on an out breath.

Now make your buttocks tight. Tense up on an in breath; hold for ten seconds; relax your muscles on an out breath.

Now tense your stomach as if to receive a punch. Tense up on an in breath; hold for ten seconds; relax your muscles on an out breath.

Now bend your elbows and tense the muscles of your arms. Tense up on an in breath; hold for ten seconds; relax your muscles on an out breath.

Now hunch your shoulders and press your head back. Tense up on an in breath; hold for ten seconds; relax your muscles on an out breath.

Now clench your jaws, frown, and screw up your eyes really tight. Tense up on an in breath; hold for ten seconds; relax your muscles on an out breath.

Now tense all your muscles together. Tense up on an in breath; hold for ten seconds; relax all your muscles on an out breath.

Stay in this position for a few minutes. If you start to become tense again, repeat the process or work just on the tense area. When you feel ready to get up, turn on your side if you are lying down or sit forward gently. Stay there for a few moments before attempting to rise.

Self-hypnosis

Self-hypnosis is a skill that can be learnt, although courses can be quite expensive. These are advertised in *Open Mind* and other publications.

Massage

Massage is a very pleasurable form of relaxation. The skilled touch of another human being can be very therapeutic. Most of us do not get enough strokes, either physical or psychological, although we may need and want them.

Think of the pleasure you can get from touch, be it holding a baby, stroking a cat or cuddling someone close. If we are tired or feeling sad we often stroke ourselves unconsciously.

We rub our eyes, run our hands through our hair, stroke our arms, hold our own hands. Touch can help us to relax and the mind knows this.

Massage is a skill you can learn so as to calm yourself in times of stress or to help someone else who is in need of some relaxation and therapeutic touch. Massaging someone else is also therapeutic because of the sense of giving, the concentration and the reciprocal sense of touch.

Courses are available that are not exorbitantly expensive and there are also self-instruction tapes and books. A good example is *Stress and Relaxation: Self-help techniques for everyone* by Jane Madders (Macdonald Optima, 1981).

Meditation

Meditation is a way of clearing the mind of all the clutter and noise it collects. It works on the basis that a relaxed mind induces a relaxed body. The most common form of meditation is through the use of mantras, that is, words or sayings that concentrate the mind.

In his book *How to Meditate*, the American psychologist Lawrence LeShan states that there are four main pathways to meditation:

1. Through the intellect – the belief being that knowledge and wisdom can be developed to a higher plane through meditation
2. Through the emotions – as in prayer
3. Through the body – by the use of exercises
4. Through action – Aikido, for example, is a form of meditation developed from the martial arts

Yoga

The main aim of yoga is to create a healthy mind in a healthy body. It has been proven scientifically to reduce tension by using a combination of postures and controlled breathing.

Although some forms of yoga are deeply spiritual and take a religious dedication to master, there are other forms that are not so demanding.

Yoga is best learnt from a qualified teacher, although it is possible to obtain books explaining postures and breathing techniques from libraries and bookshops. Many adult education centres offer classes at reasonable prices with discounts for people who are unemployed.

Eleven ways to deal with tension

Tension and anxiety are normal reactions to events in our lives which threaten our well-being. Such threats can come from accidents, financial troubles, problems on the job or in the family. How we deal with these pressures has a lot to do with our mental and emotional health. The following are 11 recommendations from the Canadian Mental Health Association:

1. *Talk it out.*
   If something is worrying you, let it out. Talk over your worries and concerns with someone you trust – husband or wife, father or mother, family doctor, clergyman, teacher or close friend. Talking relieves the strain and helps you bring problems into perspective.

2. *Run away for a while.*
   Don't spend all your time worrying about your problems. Escape for a while into a book, a movie, a game. True, 'escapism' can be overdone, but occasional breaks will help you see things more clearly.

3. *Work off your anger.*
   Give your emotions a rest by switching to physical activities. Dig the garden. Clean out the garage. Start a building project or hobby.

4. *Give in occasionally.*
   If you find yourself getting into frequent quarrels, stand your ground only when you're sure you're right. Make allowances sometimes for the fact that the other person might be right. It's easier on your system to give in now and then.

5. *Give something of yourself.*
Doing things for others can take your mind off your own problems. And you'll have a feeling of satisfaction and accomplishment.

6. *Tackle one thing at a time.*
If your workload seems unbearable, do the most urgent jobs one at a time. Put all the others aside for the time being.

7. *Don't try to be perfect.*
There are things you like to do best and things that give you the most satisfaction. Give yourself a pat on the back for those you do well, but don't try to get into *The Guinness Book of Records* with everything you do.

8. *Ease up on your criticism.*
Don't expect too much of others. Try to remember that each person has their own strengths, their own shortcomings.

9. *Don't be too competitive.*
Often co-operation is the best approach. When you give other people a break, you often make things easier for yourself, too. If they no longer feel threatened by you, they stop being a threat to you.

10. *Make the first move.*
Sometimes we have the feeling that we are being left out, slighted or rejected by others. This could be just our imagination. If you make the first move, very often others will respond.

11. *Have some fun.*
Too much work can be harmful. Old-fashioned play is essential for good physical and mental health. Everyone should have a sport, hobby or outside interest that provides a complete break from the work routine.

Psychiatric Nursing, May–June 1980

Healthy bodies, healthy minds

Maintaining our mental well-being in modern times is quite an art form, given the pressures on us to indulge in unhealthy pursuits. Overindulging in alcohol and junk food whilst avoiding exercise can work against our mental well-being, despite the fact many people use these methods to make themselves feel better. And in the long term, such habits can have serious consequences for our physical and mental health.

Alcohol

'The door to alcoholism is not forced open by a determined and suicidal few but lies open and may be inadvertently entered by any social drinker,' writes Jack Lyttle in his book *Mental Disorder* (Baillière Tindall, 1986), a warning that is so true.

Despite popular opinion, alcohol is, in fact, a depressant, and its overuse or abuse can have a devastating effect on an individual and their ability to work and have healthy, happy relationships.

The sooner a drinking problem is recognised, the easier it is to get out from under it. Below are some questions that will help you learn how dependent you are on drinking. This is a time to be absolutely honest with yourself – only you can know how seriously you are being hurt by the role alcohol plays in your life.

1. Has someone close to you sometimes expressed concern about your drinking?
2. When faced with a problem, do you often turn to alcohol for relief?

3. Are you sometimes unable to meet home or work responsibilities because of drinking?
4. Have you ever required medical attention as a result of drinking?
5. Have you ever come in conflict with the law in connection with your drinking?
6. Have you often failed to keep promises you have made to yourself about controlling or cutting out your drinking?

If you have answered yes to any of the above questions, your drinking is probably affecting your life in some major ways and you should do something about it – before it gets worse.

National Institute on Alcohol Abuse and Alcoholism

Knowing how much you drink

Considering how long alcohol has been around, it is surprising how many myths still exist. It is still widely believed that people cannot become alcoholics if they only drink beer and yet the alcohol content of a half a pint of ordinary strength lager has the same alcohol content as a single ($\frac{1}{6}$ gill) measure of gin, whisky, vodka or any other spirit; the same alcohol content as a glass of wine, a small glass of sherry or a measure of vermouth or other aperitif. So statements such as 'I can drink lager all night and it has no effect on me, but I get really drunk on whisky' need to be examined closely. For a guideline as to how much alcohol is in each drink and how much is consider safe, see the table below.

Alcohol units per drink

Drink	Measure	Units
Beers and lagers		
Ordinary strength beer or lager	$\frac{1}{2}$ pint	1
	1 pint	2
	1 can	$1\frac{1}{2}$
Export beer	1 pint	$2\frac{1}{2}$
	1 can	2

Drink	Measure	Units
Strong ale or lager	½ pint	2½
	1 pint	4
	1 can	3
Extra strength beer or lager	½ pint	2½
	1 pint	5
	1 can	4

Ciders

Average cider	½ pint	1½
	1 pint	3
	quart bottle	6
Strong cider	½ pint	2
	1 pint	4
	quart bottle	8

Spirits

	1 standard single measure in most of England and Wales (⅙ gill)	1
	1 standard single measure in Northern Ireland (¼ gill)	1½
	⅕ gill measure	1¼
	¼ gill measure served in some parts of Scotland	1½
	1 bottle	30

Table wine

(including cider wine and barley wine)

	1 standard glass	1
	1 bottle	7
	1 litre bottle	10

Sherry and fortified wine

	1 standard small measure	1
	1 bottle	12

How much should you drink?

From a mental health viewpoint this is a slightly complicated question to answer.

The recommended 'sensible' limit according to the Health Education Authority is for men up to 21 units a week, for women up to 14 units a week, spread throughout the week. This allows for two or three enjoyable evenings out with friends without seriously damaging your liver! However, if you are sitting at home or alone in a bar miserably drinking, say four gin and tonics or three pints of beer, then you are in danger of an increased risk of depression. This is because although alcohol acts as a stimulant at first it is in fact a depressant and will act upon the central nervous system in a way that will lower, rather than elevate your mood as well as affecting your judgement, skills and self-control.

Diet

The importance of diet is underplayed in all aspects of mental health except where it is part of an obvious problem such as anorexia. Diet can play a major part in mental health matters.

Some foods and drinks, for instance, are able to give your metabolic system quite a jolt. Coffee is well known for containing the stimulant caffeine, but it is perhaps less well known that tea, soft drinks, particularly of the cola variety, chocolate, sugar, salt and man-made food (E) additives can also stimulate the mind and body. In short, some foods can be mood affecting. Tension, fatigue and irritability can also be caused by the consumption of large quantities of sugar, and salt increases nervous tension, fluid retention and the level of your blood pressure.

Given that these foodstuffs can cause these reactions in someone whose mental health is OK, imagine the problems it could cause for a person suffering from anxiety, as it exacerbates their existing symptoms.

If you find that your mood fluctuates several times a day or even over a period of a few days, it might be worth while keeping a diet/mood diary to see if a pattern emerges between certain foodstuffs and your mood swings. If you find that your mood does alter after meals containing certain foodstuffs, you could run a home trial to see if the pattern repeats itself if you have the same foodstuffs on a regular basis.

Try varying your diet and particularly including raw vegetables and fruit and see how this improves your feeling of well-being.

A healthy diet

If you are unsure as to whether or not your diet is considered healthy, then ask your GP for advice. They may well refer you to the health authority dietician.

In the meantime, health educators advise that you avoid 'junk' foods and high-calorie snacks, despite the short-term energy high that they may give you. Also avoid eating a diet with a high proportion of animal fats and dairy products and try where possible to increase your intake of raw vegetables, and fruits as well as pulses.

You will find that after a period of taking a more healthy diet your system will feel noticeably sluggish if you return to a burgers and chips type menu for even a day.

It is now widely suggested that foodstuffs with a range of additives should be avoided as they can cause reactions in some people such as the well-publicised hyperactivity in children. It is recommended that the main additives to avoid are tartrazine and related food colourings. The main E numbers to be avoided are: E102, 104, 107, 110, 122, 123, 128, 151, 154, 155 and 180. Some E numbers, however, are natural colourings, such as those numbered from E160 to E170. In some products the E numbers are not displayed and so it might well be safer to avoid products that have any additives or preservatives if you have any suspicion that these may be causing you problems.

Another way of checking to see if particular foods or drinks are causing you problems is to see someone specialising in allergies.

Organic foodstuffs are still relatively expensive, so if you cannot afford to purchase them or your local shops do not stock them, if you have a garden, even a small one, you may find it worth learning organic gardening methods and producing your own healthy fruit and veg.

If all of these options are out of the question, then the following basic rules may help you to cut down your intake of questionable substances:

- Always scrub fruit, salad stuffs and vegetables that are to be eaten unpeeled.
- Although much of the goodness lies just beneath the skin of root vegetables, peeling these will help you get rid of some of the absorbed pesticides and chemical nutrients.
- Filter your water.
- Build some wholegrains and pulses into your diet.

Exercise

We all have a thousand and one excuses for not taking exercise – I'm too tired, it's boring, I haven't got time, I haven't got the energy, I'm no good at sport, I'm not fit enough (well of course you're not, you don't take enough exercise!), I need to lose weight first (you need to burn up calories by taking exercise!).

But it is a fact of life that exercise is essential for our well-being, and that goes for our mental as well as our physical health (given the extent to which these two can be separated).

Exercise works to improve our physical and mental well-being because:

- It tones up our bodies, making us look healthier and therefore more attractive, which in turn helps us to feel good about ourselves.
- It makes us feel less tired by improving the efficiency of our heart and circulatory system.
- It stimulates chemicals in our bodies that give us a 'lift', making us feel more positive and less depressed.
- It improves our appetite and digestion.
- It strengthens our bodies, our minds and our confidence.
- It provides an outlet for tension and frustration and helps us to relax.
- It gives us a feeling of healthy tiredness and helps us sleep better.

- It plays an essential part in preventing physical illnesses such as heart disease and osteoporosis (bone-thinning, a major cause of fractures and deaths in the elderly, particularly women).

There are many different forms of exercise and any exercise is better than none. Walking, running, playing team games, badminton, swimming, aerobics, dancing, yoga, tennis, bowls, golf, weight-training, martial arts – the list is endless.

Perhaps the first things to bear in mind when considering taking up exercise are safety, suitability and satisfaction.

Safety

Your GP or a reputable health and leisure instructor, perhaps at your local health centre, will help you to understand your current level of fitness and give you some indication of the type of exercise it would be safe for you to start with. Swimming for instance is excellent for building up suppleness, stamina and strength without placing too great a strain on the heart, whereas trying to run or jog a few miles when overweight, out of condition and without guidelines on how to warm up your muscles first will only result in problems that could have long-term consequences.

Be kind to yourself. Accept it will take time and perseverance to reach a satisfactory level of fitness and that a few aches and pains might be experienced at the start.

Suitability and satisfaction

If you really hate jogging then there is little point in forcing yourself out on to the streets pounding tarmac for hours on end. Start with whatever you might enjoy most.

Exercise should fit into your lifestyle and not dominate it. A busy mother at home with children may be lucky enough to have a local aerobics group with a creche or a supportive friend or relative. However, if these are not available, a home exercise programme available on video, in books or even on tape might be a solution, as might home exercise equipment which can take the form of stationary bikes, rowing machines, weights and even 'mini-gyms'. Elderly people are less likely to take to the squash courts, but swimming, brisk walking and bowls will provide a level of exercise that will vastly improve well-being, and, as fitness improves, other, more energetic activities might be attempted.

Suppleness, stamina and strength

Exercise works to build up the three 'S's – suppleness, stamina and strength.

Suppleness
Suppleness is important as exercise can place a strain on your muscles, ligaments and tendons. If these are not supple or pliable then you are far more likely to experience aches and pains. Gentle stretching should be a part of any exercise programme and a precursor to any sport.

Stamina
Stamina is your ability to keep going without having to stop to catch your breath. If you have had to run for a bus recently then you will have some idea of your level of stamina. If you have to sprint for a bus and it takes several minutes before your breathing gets back to normal then your stamina level may well need building up.

Strength
In order to meet some of the physical demands placed upon us, such as lifting children, moving furniture or even protecting ourselves, it is necessary to build up our strength. By using light weights or weight machines on a carefully designed programme it is possible not only to build up strength but also to improve muscle tone, thereby looking younger and fitter.

Motivation

All the opportunity in the world is of no use if your motivation to improve your physical fitness is not there. Some people are enormously motivated. You may well see them out jogging in the pouring rain or thrashing around a squash court in a heatwave. However, most of us experience peaks and troughs in our motivation to do most things, even those we really enjoy, particularly if they take effort.

If your motivation to take exercise is really very low most of the time, then it might help to set up a positive reward system for yourself, say, a long lie-in on Sunday if you have exercised for half an hour on Saturday. The odd cream cake or drink won't do you any harm either. Remember that allowing yourself treats is in fact good for you.

Getting a good night's sleep

Sleeplessness (insomnia) or restless nights can be a source of a great deal of distress for many people. An easy answer might seem to be sleeping tablets (hypnotics). However, drug-induced sleep is neither as healthy nor as refreshing as a deep natural sleep and so it is well worth trying other methods first. Medication should only be used as a last resort and then only for as short a time as possible.

The main indication that you have a sleeping problem is if you feel tired and unrefreshed first thing in the morning. If this is the case, then you need to understand what might be causing the sleeping problem:

- Activity – the less active we are, the less we tend to tire ourselves (although boredom can be exhausting). Try to think of a time when you have engaged in a physically tiring activity like playing squash, running or gardening and remember how sleepy you felt particularly after a relaxing bath or a glass of wine (one tot will relax you and help you sleep, more than this may add to your sleep problems). Intellectual activities are also very tiring, but we can find it hard to switch our minds off, causing tension and difficulty in sleeping. If you find that your mind is racing with ideas and problems chasing each other around in your head, try writing your thoughts down on paper.
- Age – as we grow older we tend to need less sleep as we become less active.
- Depression – early waking, between the hours of 3 o'clock

and 5 o'clock in the morning, is an indication of depression, particularly if other symptoms are present (*see* page 19). Difficulty in getting to sleep at night may well be a sign of anxiety (*see* page 13). However, there may be no underlying cause but very practical reasons that can be dealt with easily once understood.

● Discomfort – an uncomfortable mattress may be something you have become used to but may well be causing you more problems than you realise.
● Noise – traffic, noisy neighbours or a snoring partner can sometimes make sleep impossible. Not only does the noise keep us awake but so does the tension we experience as we get increasingly irritated and anxious about feeling too tired to face the next day's agenda. If you cannot do anything about the source of the problem, then earplugs might prove the answer.
● Tension – this can be caused by any number of things, but can be tackled through deep muscle relaxation (*see* page 50), listening to music, taking a bath, having a hot milky drink or reading a good novel. It is best to experiment and find your own way of winding down.

Sleeping tablets may at times be necessary in the short term, but for both a healthy body and a healthy mind, understanding and dealing with the causes of sleeplessness will often bring the greatest rewards.

Staying well

Keeping ourselves well is sometimes very difficult given the pressures of twentieth-century living. However, there are plenty of sources of advice – magazines, TV, GPs, health visitors – the list is endless.

What is more difficult to deal with are issues like homelessness, poverty, disability and other things seemingly beyond our control. To tackle these threats to health it is often necessary to work with others, for instance, as a member of a mental health or other pressure group (such as Mind). Your local Citizen's Advice Bureau or Voluntary Services Group should have a list of local groups and organisations.

4

Growing good? A guide to therapy

I speak as a person who for 12 years has suffered from mental health problems. Sometimes confused, isolated, lonely; sometimes manic, aggressive, angry; sometimes in hospital or attending day-centres or walking in the streets, on and off drugs, in and out of work; but mostly searching, seeking to understand, to sort out and find some way of contributing – to find meaning in a society which to me seems totally irrational . . .

In therapy I see the relationship between images and powerful feelings; these feelings which can threaten to be unmanageable, become accessible – and acceptable – through images.

'A Penny for your Thoughts', *Open Mind* No. 28,
August/September 1987

What exactly does therapy entail? And what types are on offer? For many years, mental health problems have been treated by drugs. For the more severe instances, drug treatment still plays a major part in a patient's care. However, it has lost a great deal of favour over the past few years and many people experiencing mental distress want alternatives. This has contributed to an increasing emphasis on psychotherapy, which allows someone to talk through their problems and related issues with a trained therapist who will help people gain a greater understanding of themselves, their strengths and weaknesses and the situation they are in, and help them find their own solutions. People may work on a one-to-one basis or in a group situation.

However, there are many different approaches to psychotherapy and some may suit needs better than another. Not all mental health problems are best treated by talking issues through. In some instances it is the situation and not the individual that should change. There are times when legal, economic or political change are the only real solution. At other times, the 'talking treatments' will be more suitable.

Choosing therapy

Psychotherapy and counselling

Both psychotherapy and counselling entail talking to someone who is trained to listen. The therapy entails a series of meetings for a specified period of time – usually 50 minutes or an hour – giving the client time and space to explore important issues. How those issues are explored depends on the therapist.

I'm afraid of the therapist. I want help, but I don't know whether to trust him. He might see things which I don't know in myself – frightening and bad elements. He seems not to be judging me, but I'm sure he is. I can't tell him what really concerns me, but I can tell him about some past experiences that are related to my concern. He seems to understand those, so I can reveal a bit more of myself.

But now I've shared with him some of this bad side of me, he despises me. I'm sure of it, but it's strange I can find little evidence of it ... It makes me feel that I want to go further, exploring me, perhaps expressing more of myself ...

But now I'm getting frightened again, and this time deeply frightened. I didn't realise that exploring the unknown recesses of myself would make me feel feelings I've never experienced before ... and now as I live these feelings in the hours with him, I feel terribly shaky, as though my world is falling apart ... yet curiously I'm eager to see him and I feel more safe when I'm with him.

I don't know who I am any more, but sometimes when I feel things I seem solid and real for a moment. I'm troubled by the contradictions I find in myself – I act one way and feel another – I think one thing and feel another. It is very disconcerting ... I feel pretty vulnerable and raw, but I know he doesn't want to hurt me, and I even believe he cares ...

You know, I feel as if I'm floating along on the current of life, very adventurously, being me ... But of course I can only do this because I feel safe in the relationship with my therapist. Or could I be myself this way outside of this relationship? I wonder. I wonder. Perhaps I could.

This passage gives an honest insight into what psychotherapy can offer someone who has a need to understand themselves – and also perhaps into what hard work is involved in personal growth and development.

There is no hard and fast distinction between counselling and psychotherapy. In general use, counselling is a talking therapy that allows people to deal with specific life issues, such as relationship difficulties or career changes, while psychotherapy is used to deal with 'deeper' issues, usually with people whose past experiences are causing them problems. However, it might be difficult to think of a 'deeper' issue than that of relationships, which are fundamental to our existence, and so rather than think of counselling as being different from psychotherapy, it might be more useful to see it as being at the slightly lighter end of a scale or continuum.

There are many different philosophies behind counselling, in the same way as there are different schools of psychotherapy, and so for the purposes of this chapter, the words 'counselling' and 'psychotherapy' will be used interchangeably.

Analytic psychotherapies

Psychoanalysis
Psychoanalysis was the first formally developed method of psychotherapy. Developed by Sigmund Freud, it concentrates upon the mental health problems that develop as a result of a battle between our inbuilt aggressive and sexual impulses (what Freud called the 'id') and our learned need to hold these

impulses in (our 'ego' and 'superego'). This internal battle, according to Freud, starts in early childhood and has the effect of preventing people from being able to cope effectively with relationships and the pressures created by their environment.

Repressed sexual and aggressive feelings are, for psychoanalysts, at the root of neuroses.

Analysis and the consequent understanding of repressed fears, it is believed, allows the individual to deal with the issues involved.

The guiding principle of psychoanalysis is *free association*. With free association a patient, or 'client', as they may more often be called, is encouraged by the analyst to give free rein to their thoughts and feelings. That is, to say whatever comes into their heads without censorship. Where a patient feels this to be impossible, they should admit to the censorship, as this is a valid part of unblocking thoughts and emotions. Imagine, just for a minute what repeating out loud exactly what comes into your head might entail saying:

Why is he asking me to say whatever comes into my head? I don't see the point. Stupid man. And he is so ugly. Expensive too. I haven't collected the damn laundry yet. It always rains on Tuesdays.

From the free association the analyst will attempt to break down blockages or resistance in thoughts and feeling and then encourage interpretation.

The idea behind this approach is that the patient is helped to discover issues of personal but hitherto unidentified importance.

The patient's relationship with the analyst is an important part of the approach. During psychoanalysis, the analyst always sits out of view of the client or patient. As the relationship develops, the patient begins to respond to the analyst in particular ways. For instance, a patient may feel very warmly towards the analyst or, alternatively, very hostile. Freud referred to this as 'transference'. His assumption was that it was an indication of feelings for significant others such as parents.

As the analysis continues patients experience therapeutic benefit through:

- abreaction
- insight
- working through

Abreaction is a term that describes the release of very strong emotions, such as anger. This may come as a result of talking about painful past experiences. The process of abreaction does not take away the memory of the original experience, but can provide a release for bottled-up emotions and also the opportunity to discover more.

The continuous exploration of experience and emotion can lead to a gradual *insight* into the source of the problems the patient is experiencing. Once this insight has been achieved it is a case of helping the patient to understand and change their responses in situations where they may be experiencing particular difficulty.

Psychoanalysis, like many of the psychoanalytic psychotherapies, aims to *work through* neuroses and therefore is felt to be unsuitable for people experiencing a psychotic disturbance, compulsive disorders (*see* Behaviour Therapy below) or addictions.

Psychoanalytic psychotherapy

Based on the principles of psychoanalysis, psychoanalytic psychotherapy differs in three fundamental ways:

- the therapist is in full view of the client (the client is unlikely to be lying down on a couch, but rather sitting on a chair facing the therapist)
- the therapist concentrates on actual life problems rather than meandering through the unconscious
- the therapist places less emphasis on the biological drives and more on the social and cultural factors that shape our lives and behaviour

However, in a similar way to psychoanalysis, psychoanalytic psychotherapy is based on the belief that unconscious motives and fears are what lie beneath most emotional problems.

Neo-Freudian analysis

There are a number of so-called neo-Freudian schools of thought in the psychoanalytic field. Led by notable personalities such as Adler, Fromm, Horney, Rank and Sullivan, these place less emphasis on Freud's libido theory (that people are driven by instinctual drives) and more on culture and the importance of interpersonal relationships. They acknowledge the importance of security and self-esteem to the individual.

One of these schools, the Sullivanian school, is currently very popular and, unlike many other forms of analytical therapy, does have something to offer people suffering from psychotic types of mental health problem.

Jungian psychotherapy

The final type of therapy based on an analytical approach is that of Carl Jung.

Jung preferred to refer to his approach as 'analytical psychology' rather than 'psychoanalysis' and for him the unconscious was not just something unique to each individual but was also shared, with common 'inherited' knowledge. This he referred to as the 'collective unconscious'.

Post-analytic one-to-one therapies

Gestalt therapy

Although the founder of Gestalt therapy, Frederick (Fritz) Perls, was himself once a Freudian training analysts, anything less like psychoanalysis than Gestalt therapy might be hard to come by.

Gestalt therapy is grounded very much in the here and now. That is, there is no exploration of the past. The emphasis is on awareness of what the individual wants and needs *now*, and on feeling.

Unlike the talking psychotherapies, Gestalt therapy places far more emphasis on the whole person. The body and how it moves and feels are just as important as the mind, its thoughts and verbal expressions.

Exploration of feelings is often done dramatically. For example a client might be asked by a Gestalt therapist to role play between themselves and a member of their family

with whom they may have some unfinished business (unresolved conflict). They may do this by using an empty chair
which they will address as if the other party is sitting there.

Primal therapy

Much further from the here and now than Dr Arthur Janov's
primal therapy it is probably difficult to get. Believing that
deeply painful childhood experiences remain with us and that
the childish fending off of pain and subsequent long-lasting
tension creates the neurosis that stays with us, for Janov the
need is to uproot this deep-seated pain and literally scream it
out.

The way in which primal therapy works, or at least how it is
structured, is different from most other types of talking
therapies. It involves the patient in removing themselves from
their ordinary lives for a period of three weeks, either by
moving into a hotel or therapy centre. They are to take no
drugs, including alcohol and cigarettes, which might ordinarily be used to reduce tension. They have a session with a
therapist each day for this period. The sessions are not defined
by any time limit and may go on for several hours or until the
therapist decides that the patient has had enough.

In each session the therapist works towards getting the
patient to express their deepest feelings towards their parents.
The concentration on the basic fear and pain, centred around
the patient's belief that they were unloved by their parents
and the trauma that caused, is intended to cut out the
transference so important in psychoanalysis. The simple truth,
as perceived by Dr Janov, is that re-experiencing those early
feelings will get rid of both the neurosis and the associated
transference.

Following the initial three-week session, clients can continue in a primal group which does not act in the same way as
other group therapies (*see below*) but is rather a cluster of
individuals pursuing their own primal experience rather than
contributing to the group and the growth of the other
participants.

Rogerian therapy

Rogerian therapy is the embodiment of the humanist

approach to psychotherapy. The Rogerian world view is a very positive one, believing that people are essentially positive, whole beings and that therapy can bring this wholeness, this good feeling, to the surface.

The belief is that the therapy works by talking things through with a therapist who is non-judgemental and who should hold the patient in unconditional positive regard, the regard being for what the person essentially is rather than what they do.

The therapist works by feeding back to the patient the words or statements that hold a key to how the patient feels about something. The idea is to help the client become aware of their self-perception, which is laced with self-hatred, and through the continued positive regard of the therapist, to see themselves in a more loving, accepting light. It is essential that the therapist's responses to the client are sincere.

The Rogerian therapeutic approach is one that is increasingly being developed and used amongst mental health professionals in the UK, particularly mental health nurses and clinical psychologists.

Biofunctional therapy
Biofunctional therapists believe that neurosis stems from a disruption in the body's ability to function naturally. They use a variety of approaches, including massage and movement, to re-establish this natural functioning.

Hypnotherapy
Hypnotherapy is associated with 'putting people to sleep' (altering their state of consciousness) and then instigating behavioural changes. As a therapy it is used to tackle certain addictions like smoking and gambling. However, hypnotherapy can also be used in a much more subtle way, by inducing a trance-like state – there is no loss of consciousness – that allows the mind to wander but in a gently directed way. As an exercise it can be very therapeutic.

Behaviour and cognitive behaviour therapies

Behaviour therapies are distinct from other types in three main ways:

1. The individual's 'problem' is seen as being distinct from them as a person; it is something separate from them but something that they 'own', or agree that they have, such as a fear of flying in aeroplanes.
2. Using methods based on learning theories behaviour therapy is directive rather than suggestive.
3. It claims to be scientific in as much as its methods and results are observable, measurable, testable and reproducible.

There has been a huge growth in the credibility and use of behaviour therapy to treat mental health problems and behaviour therapists claim something like a 90 per cent success rate. However, although this looks very impressive on paper, it must be remembered that behaviour therapists select their clients on the basis of their suitability for behaviour therapy, which must improve their chances of success enormously.

Behaviour therapy is not designed to help the client understand why they are behaving in a particular way, but to change the existing behaviour by retraining, by learning more appropriate behaviour in given situations.

Several techniques are used by behaviour therapists and these should be selected according to the individual patient's needs:

- *Assertiveness training*
  This is now so popular, it is probably not recognised by many people as being a form of behaviour therapy. However, it is widely used to help people deal with difficult everyday situations, such as dealing with a difficult boss, taking faulty goods back to a shop and generally helping them to assert themselves when faced with a person or situation that can be adverse to their general mental health.

- *Aversion therapy*
  The aim of this technique is to get the patient to associate their unwanted behaviour with an unpleasant experience.

A simple example that many parents have probably tried is painting a child's nails with bitter almonds in an attempt to stop a nail-biting habit.

Giving someone with an alcohol problem a drug called Antabuse, which makes them feel very sick if they drink alcohol, is another example. Obviously the patient or client's consent to this type of treatment is essential to its success.

- *Contracts*
This is simply an agreement between two or more people to try and change a behaviour pattern. Success or failure is discussed with the therapist at following sessions.

- *Desensitisation*
This is often used in situations where a person has an exaggerated fear of something, such as flying or spiders. The person is helped to relax and then is very gently and gradually exposed to what they fear. In the case of fear of spiders, the person may initially be shown a photograph of a spider followed by a toy spider. This process would continue until the person felt able to be confronted by and even touch a real spider. This gradual exposure is very different from flooding or implosion.

- *Flooding or implosion*
With this method a person is (with their consent) confronted with their fear and is then assisted to deal with the feelings of anxiety or panic that follow. For instance, someone with a fear of open spaces would be taken to the middle of a very large field and someone with a fear of spiders would probably have several dumped in their lap. It is hoped that in this way the person will learn that they will survive the event with (hopefully) no lasting ill effects. This approach is used more widely in the United States than in the United Kingdom, although its popularity is waning.

- *Modelling*
In this approach the therapist models the desired behaviour.

● *Operant conditioning*
  This is a sort of opposite to aversion therapy, whereby a person is rewarded for 'good' behaviour. For someone suffering from anorexia, this type of approach is used to encourage eating. Parents often use operant conditioning to motivate children to behave well, particularly in public.

● *Paradoxical intention*
  This works in a rather peculiar way, as the patient is encouraged to produce the symptom and then told to make it worse. This has the paradoxical effect of getting rid of the symptom.

In cognitive behaviour therapies, the patient learns methods for increasing positive thoughts and decreasing negative thoughts, for identifying 'irrational' thoughts and challenging them; and for using self-instructions (self-talk) to help handle problem situations.

Group therapy

Because many people find that their greatest difficulty is in how they relate to other people, it can be of particular benefit for them to work through some of their difficulties in a group therapy setting.

The therapeutic factors are believed to be:

● *Acceptance*
  The sense of belonging, being supported, cared for and valued by the group – in particular, being accepted even when someone has revealed something about themselves which they themselves regarded as unacceptable. Especially important in the early stages of group membership.

● *Self-disclosure*
  Revealing previously hidden personal information about oneself to the group. Not to be equated with high participation or with dramatic openness.

- *Catharsis*
  Emotional release leading to relief – ventilating feelings (positive or negative) about life events or other group members.

- *Learning from interpersonal actions*
  Making an effort to relate in a constructive way to the group, either by initiating behaviour or responding to other group members. The person's attempt to change their way of relating is more important than the reactions of the other members.

- *Self-understanding (insight)*
  The person learns something important about their behaviour, their assumptions or their motivation. This can come about through feedback, confrontation or interpretation by the rest of the group.

- *Universality*
  Seeing that other group members have similar problems and feelings, reduces the person's sense of being unique or alone.

- *Altruism*
  The person feels better about themselves because they learn that they can be of value to others and they improve their own self-image by helping other group members.

- *Vicarious learning*
  The person experiences something of value for themselves by observing other group members.

- *Guidance*
  The person receives useful factual information or instruction from the group leader, or advice and suggestions from other group members.

- *Instillation of hope*
  Seeing that other members improve gives the person a sense of optimism about their own potential for progress.

Family therapy

Most therapies concentrate on the individual and work with them to discover and deal with various 'blockages' to personal development and growth. However, it was recognised that while individual therapy seemed to have a beneficial effect for many people, they experienced a relapse or re-experience of old problems once they returned to their family setting. This, along with the growing interest in systems, led to the development of family therapy.

In the family therapy setting, brothers, sisters, mother and father are all included. In fact, some therapists like to include the extended family, and so grandparents and even aunts and uncles can be involved.

The belief behind family therapy is that the mental health problem shown by the person who has become the patient is only a sign that there is something not operating in an ideal way within the family. It is the family system that is causing the problem.

The way in which family therapy works is quite complex and may seem very threatening to those involved. The family sits in a room with a therapist who will question actions and reactions of various family members. However, because the therapist, albeit temporarily, becomes involved in the system, there needs to be independent observers who can watch the whole proceedings without being in the same room and therefore affecting proceedings. The way this is accomplished is to have a large two-way mirror in the therapy room through which the observers can see what is going on. They are able to talk to the therapist in the room and suggest questions that they might ask of one or more of the family.

All this is, of course, carried out with the full co-operation of family members who are involved to the point of agreeing to the members of the team who will act as observers.

In other situations, the family may work with two therapists, usually a male and female, in the family home. It is also possible for therapists to videotape the family during their therapy session in order to allow family members to witness second-hand certain important, perhaps destructive, interactions.

Family therapy is believed to be of particular benefit to

people who suffer from a schizophrenic-type mental health problem.

Marital therapy

'Marital' therapy is now an outdated term as more and more people set up long-term relationships outside the marriage bond. This has been recognised by the largest relationship counselling organisation in the UK, Relate, who used to go under the title of the Marriage Guidance Council.

However it is termed, for marital or relationship therapy to be successful, both partners need to be involved.

Although approaches differ, the main emphasis is on getting partners to reach more understanding of each other's needs, to help them communicate their feelings more effectively to each other and to find effective strategies for resolving their conflicts.

Sex therapy and psycho-sexual counselling

This is usually but not always a specialist area of relationship therapy. The reason why I say 'usually but not always' is because there is a tendency to overlook the fact that people outside an intimate relationship may define a need for therapy, particularly, but not exclusively, if they are experiencing some difficulty in coming to terms with their sexuality and how this expresses itself. This therapy is offered in the form of psycho-sexual counselling.

Self-help groups

One of the worst feelings when you are suffering from any mental health problem, be it loneliness, alcoholism, depression or a schizophrenic-type illness, is that you are alone. Because of the fear and ignorance around mental health problems, gaining support from your local community or even some of your friends may prove very difficult. In any case, if the people around you have not had your experience it may prove very difficult for them to empathise and be supportive. Depressed people may be told to pull themselves together. Unless someone suffers with alcoholism, they may find it impossible to understand the craving for drink or the horrors of withdrawal symptoms. It is not only sufferers who need support and understanding. Relatives also need someone to talk to.

Self-help groups let people know that they are not alone. There are very many such groups, which have come together for a multitude of reasons, to meet a multitude of needs. Alcoholics Anonymous, perhaps the best known, has over a million members.

Of course, one of the reasons people avoid joining a self-help group is that they have to admit openly that they need help. They have to admit they are vulnerable. Carers particularly feel terribly guilty at times when they feel that they just cannot cope any more, or even just do not want to. But joining any self-help group is not a sign of weakness. Just the opposite. It is a sign of great strength.

If you want to know about any local self-help groups, you can check with your GP practice, library or local newspaper. Also, by contacting the national branch of the appropriate group you may well receive support and advice for setting up your own local group. *See* Useful Addresses section.

Choosing a therapist

When it comes to choosing therapy there is a growing feeling that the choice of therapist is as important, if not more so, than the type of therapy employed. This is particularly important in the talking therapies.

It is not advised that you allow well-meaning friends to provide counselling, as the professional detachment and clear boundaries are very important to a healing relationship.

Checking a therapist's credentials

There are no nationally recognised qualifications for counsellors and psychotherapists, though there are many diplomas and certificates, and there are professional organisations. Some people have no formal qualifications at all, but this does not make them poor therapists – having the right personality and useful experience of life can be as useful. The most important skill the counsellor has is the ability to listen.

If you have a choice of therapists it is a good idea to see several before you make up your mind and to get a recommendation if possible.

It is usual to have an initial interview so that the therapist can decide if they can help you and you can decide if you want to see them. Do not be afraid to ask any questions about their training, experience or approach, including what professional organisations they belong to, whether they receive supervision for their work, what payment arrangements are to be made, whether it is a totally confidential service and whether they have had therapy themselves.

The most important question to ask is of yourself: 'Can I have a good relationship with this person?'

At present, most counsellors and psychotherapists are white and middle-class and they may not have a good understanding of people from other backgrounds. However, there are some organisations which offer talking treatments especially to black people and people from minority ethnic communities. Gender, social background and sexuality can all play a part in whether you are comfortable with your therapist.

If you see someone privately, the British Association for Counselling (BAC) list the training and qualifications of their members in their *Counselling and Psychotherapy Resources Directory*. The United Kingdom Council for Psychotherapy, which represents over 70 psychotherapy organisations, also provides access to information about accredited psychotherapists.

If you do not see a therapist privately, you may have no choice about whom you see, but you are still entitled to ask about their training, qualifications, experience and approach.

Some therapists may be more effective than others or one may particularly suit you. However, your own attitude will also make a difference. If you are determined to make the most of every session and be completely honest about yourself, it is more likely to work. The therapist cannot do everything for you. Research suggests that the most important ingredient for success is that you and the counsellor have a good relationship with each other.

How to judge whether therapy is working

Therapy can bring about an immediate improvement or the change may be more gradual. One way of recording your progress is to keep a diary.

A good therapist will regularly check that the client is benefiting and will suggest ending the sessions if not.

Many people report that their problems do not go away during therapy but that they feel relieved about sharing them and better able to cope.

What to do if you feel abused

In therapy you will reveal a lot about yourself while learning little about the therapist, so it is easy to feel that they are stronger and more powerful. This can leave you vulnerable to exploitation. It is an unfortunate truth that some counsellors and psychotherapists do get into abusive relationships with their clients.

This can happen in a number of ways, such as emotional abuse by being unreliable or encouraging dependency. Financial abuse can occur through encouraging clients to stay in therapy when they are no longer benefiting.

Carrying out research or new techniques without the consent of the client, using the client's time to talk about their own problems and imposing their own values on the client are other forms of abuse, as are boundary breaking, by giving one client's home address to another, betrayal of confidentiality, or by the therapist deliberately seeing a client outside therapy, the worst case being the setting up of a sexual relationship. Under no condition should therapists have a sexual relationship with clients. Even if the client wants such a relationship, the desire may arise from transference feelings, and it is the responsibility of the therapist to maintain appropriate boundaries.

If you are dissatisfied with your therapy, remember that you are a customer. You have a right to discuss practical arrangements with your therapist, review how your sessions are going or to air a grievance. You can always leave.

If you want to take matters further, you can lodge a complaint.

If the therapist is working within the NHS or for any other agency, there should be a written complaints procedure. For private patients, the BAC have a written complaints procedure which applies to their members. All member organisations of the UKCP are also required to have a UKCP-approved complaints procedure.

A successful complaint should result in the therapist being barred from membership of their relevant organisation, but as there is no statutory registration of therapists, they may still be able to practise.

If you are seeing a therapist who is not a member of a professional body, then there are unfortunately few options for redress. If an assault has taken place, a criminal action may be brought by the police, otherwise the client could consult a solicitor about bringing a civil action for damages, based on the therapist's possible breach of 'duty of care' to the client. However, both these avenues are problematic. It is important to consider what outcome you would like before beginning a complaints procedure. An apology might sometimes be enough. If not, and you encounter difficulties, support is available from organisations such as Mind and the Prevention of Professional Abuse Network (*see* Useful Addresses).

Availability of therapy

Psychoanalysis is not available on the NHS. The main reason for this is that the cost would be exorbitant. Analysis requires an individual to have at least three sessions a week with a psychoanalyst over a period of three to five years. These sessions can cost in excess of £100 per session! The likeliest place to find a psychoanalyst is in London, probably in Harley Street.

Psychotherapy and counselling may be available from your local health services, either through your GP or community mental health centre. Some voluntary agencies such as Relate (formerly the Marriage Guidance Council), CRUSE (for bereavement) and Open Door (specifically for young people) offer counselling, as do other organisations, for example the Westminster Pastoral Foundation.

There are private counsellors and psychotherapists who

offer their services at a price, which may vary from £5 to £45. Some offer a sliding scale according to income.

Some employers offer access to counselling through employee assistance programmes, which can put people in touch with therapists and counsellors and often pay for some sessions.

Schools and colleges often have counsellors or access to a counselling service. Where universities offer counselling courses there are often a number of trainee counsellors looking for clients.

However, for people who have suffered from a mental health problem that is not believed suitable for therapy, the struggle to gain access to such a service may be very difficult and sometimes futile. The writer of 'A Penny for your Thoughts' had problems gaining access to therapy. After being directed to the Arbours Association (*see* Useful Addresses), she committed herself to one therapy session a week at £8 a time. As she got in touch with more difficult feelings, she increased the therapy sessions to two per week – a total of £16. At this time (1984) she was receiving £41.60 in benefits a week and her fees made a sizeable hole in her funds. The Department of Health (and Social Security as it was then) would not help her by allowing her benefit to support therapy as a treatment, although it would have proved much cheaper than treating her with medication and hospitalisation. She risked debt and disappointment over a very long period of time to fight for something she believed was her right. Her courage was tremendous.

To be Picasso and paint a person with three viewpoints simultaneously is art. To be Wordsworth and wander lonely as a cloud is poetry. To be an ordinary person and talk about feelings symbolically is schizophrenia.

Surviving community care

'Community care' is the term used for the 'new wave' approach to mental health care provision. It refers to the closing down of large-scale Victorian institutions with their miles of echoing corridors and sad, shuffling feet going nowhere. It is an acknowledgement of the stultifying effect on the human soul caused by incarceration in impersonal institutions that take away rather than build upon the living skills of people with long-term mental health problems.

When we talk of mental health services there is a tendency to think of psychiatrists, hospitals and not a great deal else. This way of thinking is firmly stuck in the so-called 'medical model', a service dominated by doctors dealing with illness. However, this approach to mental health care and service provision is now a thing of the past. In fact, many mental health services and providers of mental health care have nothing to do with hospitals or even the National Health Service.

Mind identifies 12 necessary conditions, or core components, to achieving effective community care:

1. Opportunities for achieving life quality
2. Personal support during a period of distress
3. Support during a personal crisis
4. Practical help at home
5. Opportunities to assure income
6. Somewhere to live or stay
7. Access to paid or unpaid occupation
8. Access to information that supports fair treatment
9. Someone to talk to
10. Opportunities for assuring mobility and travel
11. Ways of improving access to and contact with services
12. Opportunities for taking a break

As the above list recognises, mental health survival depends on a great many things.

For a woman who is isolated at home with young children, it may depend upon friendly neighbours, a local playgroup, access to good transport and a supportive partner.

For people who have had a long period in a psychiatric hospital it can be the ability to cope with everyday things like shopping, cooking, making a telephone call or building a social life. After having had most of the decisions about these things taken away from them, developing life skills becomes essential to their mental health survival.

For a newly retired woman who has worked all her adult life, mental health survival may depend on her ability to make the transition from a life of work to a life of recreation. She may need to learn to structure her own time and to make new friends.

For someone who experiences recurring bouts of depression, mental health survival may depend on building a good prevention strategy, ensuring a healthy, regular diet, sufficient exercise and positive thinking.

For most of us financial security plays an important part in our mental health.

Whatever it takes to ensure our mental health, one thing is certain: we cannot do this without help.

The people who are best at surviving life's 'little dilemmas' are the ones who are able to get help when they need it. They seem to be skilled at finding out what is available and are not too proud to ask for help.

Asking for help is something that in our culture we find difficult to do. Hiding our feelings, coping by ourselves, not needing others – for some strange reason these seem to be extolled as virtues. But while it may not do to be crying on everyone's shoulder all the time, or to allow ourselves to be totally dependent on others and refuse to fend for ourselves, there seems to be some reluctance to pitch into the middle ground. There are people and organisations who enjoy trying to help others, to provide a service that is very much needed – and there is some skill in finding and approaching them.

Help can come in a variety of ways. Support groups,

telephone helplines, counselling services, social groups and the statutory services provided by the health and social services are around for people who need them and know how to access them.

Finding support

This book can only provide a very general guide to advice and support and individual needs vary widely. For this reason it is important that you have a good idea what support services are available in your area. Your local Citizen's Advice Bureau is a good starting-point, as is your nearest large library. Ideally, your local health authority and social services departments can be helpful, although it is sometimes difficult to get through to the right person and some local authorities are more helpful than others. Your local Mind office may be able to offer leaflets and guidance.

If you are being discharged from in-patient psychiatric care, you should have your needs assessed by the local health and social services. Under a system called the care programme approach, one or more care professionals should discuss your needs from your point of view and theirs, with a view to agreeing follow-up care when you are discharged from hospital. Your needs may range from one-to-one counselling alone, through to monitoring medication, help with housing, finances, work and providing support. The 'care package' that is agreed to help meet your needs on discharge should be co-ordinated by your 'keyworker' (an identified care professional, ideally with whom you will already have a good relationship, such as a community psychiatric nurse or social worker). The effectiveness of this care should be monitored by your keyworker with you and reviewed at least every six months.

The care programme approach should be available to all patients discharged from psychiatric in-patient care, whether they were voluntary patients or not. However, for some people, such as those who have been held in hospital under Section 3 of the Mental Health Act 1983 and discharged under Section 117, or those with an exceptionally high need for support and monitoring discharged under a supervision order, the care programme approach still applies, but is a legal requirement as well as good practice and an expectation. Chapter 6 deals with supervised discharge, supervision registers and mental health rights in more detail while the rest of this chapter looks at some of the services that should be available to people as part of community care.

Accommodation

Shelter is a basic need, and yet it is firmly in the grip of a market economy that means too many people live in inadequate housing or may even become homeless.

From a mental health perspective, decent, reasonably priced accommodation is vital for the following reasons:

- It gives us warmth, shelter and security.
- It allows us to express ourselves.
- It is a place to bring friends.
- It allows us to share our lives in a family situation if we wish.
- It gives us a secure base from which to venture into perhaps less safe territory.
- It may give us a sense of pride and add to our self-esteem.
- It gives us an address – very important if we need to claim unemployment benefit.
- If we live alone, it can give us privacy, although it might also isolate us from others and make us lonely.
- If we share our accommodation it can give us companionship, although it may detract from our need for privacy.

The nature and quality of our accommodation is therefore very important to our overall mental as well as physical well-being. Of course, there are people who choose not to tie themselves to accommodation because of the associated responsibilities of cost, conformity and company. However, these are perhaps a small proportion of the homeless, many of whom have had to leave homes or accommodation that provided few of the benefits listed above. For others it is often nothing more than the lack of availability of affordable housing as, unfortunately, our capitalist economy means that our most basic needs are often the costliest to fulfil.

For people whose accommodation situation is a particular

issue for them because their existing situation is detrimental to their mental health, there are some organisations that can help:

- Shelter is a national organisation with local branches to help people find accommodation.
- Housing associations provide decent accommodation at reasonable rents and are a good alternative to local authority housing, although the demand for both is high.
- YMCAs offer short-term accommodation.
- Organisations such as the Elderly Accommodation Counsel Ltd, Age Concern and Help the Aged can offer advice and guidance for elderly people needing more appropriate accommodation. If it is a care home that is needed, then the British Federation of Care Home Proprietors or the National Confederation of Registered Residential Care Homes Associations are worth contacting.
- Short-term shelter is provided by organisations such as the Salvation Army.

For people who have become homeless after a long period in a psychiatric hospital, suitable housing should be arranged by the hospital with a social worker or perhaps a specially appointed accommodation officer. The choices are:

- Lodgings with a family who let a room in their house.
- Sheltered flats or bed-sitting rooms which are for those most able to live independent lives.
- Hostels, some of which provide support for residents with previous mental health problems and some which provide only basic bed and breakfast.
- Group homes, which are usually run by social services, voluntary organisations or health authorities. These vary in size and professional support is provided in line with the needs of the residents.

However, it may well be that 'official' housing is not something you are happy with, believe you need or perhaps the choice made on your behalf (although you have a right to be involved in any decision made about your future) is not a good one for you. If this is the case, then you may wish to take control of your own housing situation. To an extent this means that you become vulnerable to the cut and thrust of market forces. If you go this route, ensure you have support from people who know their way around the housing arena.

As well as Shelter and the housing associations, check your local *Yellow Pages* and Citizen's Advice Bureau for local housing schemes.

There are a number of national and regional organisations that offer accommodation for people who have been in hospital because of their mental health problems (*see* Useful Addresses). These include:

- The Arbours Association, which has long-stay houses in London run on a therapeutic community basis.
- Guideposts, a project-based service which provides accommodation for ex-patients supported by a social worker and community mental health nurse as well as local volunteers.
- The Mental After Care Association, which covers southeast England and provides half-way accommodation (i.e. a stepping-stone to more permanent individual accommodation) and residential care for people over 65 and for those who need greater support and some respite care to allow people who care for those with high dependency mental health problems like Alzheimer's disease to have a break.
- The Psychiatric Rehabilitation Association, which provides accommodation in London on a group or more individual basis (known as 'cluster' flats). They also have an intensive care accommodation section which is staffed for people who may be experiencing a mental health crisis but who do not need hospital care.
- Local Mind schemes, which have advice and contacts that are invaluable to people experiencing accommodation difficulties.
- The St Mungo Housing Scheme, which exists to 'improve the quality of life for single homeless people by providing accommodation and support services to help them progress towards greater self-sufficiency and, where possible, independence in the community'. This is based in London.
- The Life Care and Housing Trust, which provides accommodation and support for unsupported pregnant women

and women with babies. Advice and other practical help is also available.

- The Richmond Fellowship, which offers residential accommodation run on a therapeutic community basis. Some of the homes are set up for people who are experiencing particular mental health problems such as those caused by schizophrenia or drug dependency.
- For information on local schemes, check your local *Yellow Pages* under Housing Associations, Societies and Trusts, your local Citizen's Advice Bureau or your local authority housing department.

For elderly people who are no longer able to live on their own and have no family support there are also choices to be made. Perhaps one of the most difficult times many of us will have to face is owning up to the fact that we are no longer able to live completely independently, that we will have to rely on others. This is difficult not only because of our pride and fear of encroaching dependence but also because as we start to lose control over our own situation we have to rely on others and the care they provide. And good and bad residential care exists in both the private and public sectors.

Your local Citizen's Advice Bureau and social services department will provide you with a list of local residential homes. Those which belong to the National Confederation of Registered Residential Care Home Associations or the British Confederation of Care Home Proprietors (*see* Useful Addresses) should follow guidelines issued by these organisations which offer more than that recommended by the government, including activities programmes.

For people who have become homeless and who are looking for shelter or accommodation, Salvation Army hostels, the YMCA and the Shelter group as well as local religious groups can offer temporary accommodation.

Employment

Because of the nature of mental health problems, the disruptive effect they can have on someone's life and the outdated attitudes of many employers, it is difficult for some people, particularly those who have repeated experiences of mental distress, to maintain full-time employment. It is hoped that the Disability Discrimination Act brought out in December 1996 will go some way to protect the rights of people with mental health problems, particularly those already in work who now have more power if they feel they are being bullied or are subject to persecution because of their mental health problems. Mind's view is that this Act, although a start, does not go far enough and tackles only some of the discrimination caused by the stigma and prejudice attached to mental health problems.

For some people it is possible to find work on an assisted scheme through such organisations as Remploy, the Psychiatric Rehabilitation Association, some local branches of Mind and the Richmond Fellowship.

However, many people want to return to full-time employment and do not wish to experience prejudice as a result of their illness. Firms employing more than 20 people are by law required to reserve 3 per cent of its posts for people registered as disabled, but whether or not an individual would see their problem as 'disabling' is debatable. A discussion with the Disablement Resettlement Officer at the local Job Centre might provide some guidance and support.

The St Mungo Housing Scheme offers hands-on skills training, employment counselling and work experience placements which helps to improve employment prospects with local employers.

It should be stressed here that a mental health problem on its own is not grounds for dismissal, although poor work performance or absenteeism for long periods of time are.

Getting to know people

Mental distress of any form often makes forming relationships that bit more difficult. And heaven knows it isn't easy for any of us. Other people can sometimes make us want to withdraw. The sheer effort of 'being social' can wear us out. But at the same time, the need for other people remains.

In order to get support on a more casual basis than from a mental health professional or practical organisation, it is necessary to build a support network. And that means getting to know people. Most social situations (ironically) are designed for people who already know people, not for people who are on their own.

Many social settings can in fact feel quite threatening. In order to make the first tentative steps towards building up new relationships it is important to make a few small, successful steps to build up confidence.

Depending on how confident you feel, you can take a number of routes:

- Local mental health organisations, such as Mind, arrange coffee mornings and other meetings such as stress management and relaxation groups. These offer the chance to meet other people and learn or practise useful health-promoting skills in an environment where you may be able to share your experiences with others who understand. If you feel you would like support from people who can associate with your experience of mental distress then you may wish to join a group such as the Schizophrenia Fellowship or Tranx.

- You may feel that you do not want to gain support from an organisation directly associated with mental health, in which case an alternative, depending on your age, sex or situation, might be more appropriate. Your local newspaper should have a list of such organisations which might include:

    Gingerbread (for single parents)
    Compassionate Friends (for bereaved parents)
    The Association of Carers (for people looking after dependent relatives)

- Voluntary organisations allow you to work as many hours as you feel able, enabling you to give something to others and to meet people at the same time. Although this is no substitute for paid employment if that is what you want and feel able to pursue, voluntary work does give a great deal. Voluntary organisations are often listed in local newspapers or can be found under Charitable and Benevolent Organisations in the *Yellow Pages*. Some towns have a voluntary work co-ordinating office and your Citizen's

Advice Bureau or local social services department should know if this is the case.

As well as the better known organisations such as the Red Cross, Oxfam and Age Concern, there are local organisations set up to help local people, as well as national campaigning organisations like the Friends of the Earth and Greenpeace.

- If you are single and feel you would like to start a relationship, then there are groups set up to allow divorced, separate and single people to meet and socialise. These are sometimes run by religious organisations but might also be set up and run by enthusiastic individuals who are fed up with a social scene dominated by couples.
- If you are able to afford it, evening and day classes are available at local colleges. As well as meeting other people, these classes can help you gain new skills or qualifications. Reduced rates are usually available for people on limited incomes.

Helplines

Perhaps the best known helpline is that operated by the Samaritans. Too readily associated solely as being an organisation for people who feel suicidal, the 'Sams' will also befriend those who are lonely and finding it difficult to ask for support elsewhere.

Health care services

Acute hospital care

Going into hospital can be a frightening experience for anyone, and because of the stigma that is still unfortunately attached to a psychiatric hospital, the event can be an extremely distressing one that may well aggravate the mental distress the person may have been admitted with in the first place. Much of this fear and stigma is attached to the old-style asylums, still referred to as 'lunatic asylums' during the early part of this century. It is no wonder that someone who is suffering from post-natal depression or who is finding it difficult to come to terms with a bereavement, who may be suffering from very frightening hallucinations or the with-drawal symptoms of alcohol or drug addiction becomes increasingly distressed at the thought of being called 'mad'.

Not all people suffering from mental health problems want to have hospital care, and in some instances they are taken into hospital against their wishes under the provisions of the Mental Health Act 1983, which lays down clear guidelines as to what rights the mental health staff have to assess and treat a patient, and what rights the patient has. However, while the Mental Health Act has an important part to play in the care of mental distress, its use can itself be very distressing, as the patient often feels criminalised. Mind also believes that many people are admitted to hospital under the Mental Health Act who do not need to be.

For many people who need intensive support, close obser-vation and careful assessment the environment of a hospital is very important. For most people the stay will be approxi-mately six weeks. Unfortunately, with psychiatric bed occu-pancy running at something like 120 per cent, people are often discharged prematurely, sometimes with tragic consequences.

With the continued closure of the old-type asylums, people are increasingly likely to be admitted to a ward in a district general hospital that specialises in mental health problems in the same way as other wards specialise in maternity services or surgical after-care.

While in hospital, the patient may well be offered therapies, including occupational therapy (*see below*), group therapy, counselling (on a one-to-one basis) and recreational excursions (for those who are well enough), as well as the chance to develop many of their practical and coping skills.

Some hospitals offer a separate rehabilitation service which is designed to reintroduce people to the community after a long hospital stay.

People needing long-term support are given this, wherever possible, in the community. If the patient does not have their own home or a family, they may be placed in a group home, hostel or lodgings depending on their needs.

There can be little argument, however, that community housing schemes are still too few and far between and there are few services that offer respite or genuine asylum (somewhere to get away from life's stresses and difficulties for a while) and that in-patient care in hospital is not the most appropriate option, merely the only one available.

Day hospitals
A day hospital offers a range of services that help people who are experiencing mental health problems but who do not need in-patient care. Patients may be involved in occupational or art therapy, group therapy or counselling, as well as having the opportunity to socialise with other people. It is probably fair to say that in a day hospital the emphasis is on skills development.

For people needing 'depot' injections (*see* Chapter 7) these may be administered at the day hospital. They are open from around 10 a.m. to 4 p.m.

Mental health centres
These tend to vary depending on the degree of progressiveness of the managers and health professionals involved. Quite often they tend to be for professionals rather than for patients. However, as more services look to consulting the users this may change. Services can include a drop-in centre, a GP, community mental health nurses, psychologists, social workers and voluntary workers.

Mental health care professionals
GP (general practitioner)
Although GPs are not traditionally seen as mental health care professionals and would not usually attend ward rounds as part of the multi-disciplinary team, they provide a great deal of mental health care, either in the short-term prescribing of anti-depressants or anti-anxiolitics or in just listening to people's emotional problems (although while some GPs are very good at finding extra time, such as double appointments, the average consultation usually lasts only a few minutes).

Hospital-based and community mental health (psychiatric) nurse
The mental health (psychiatric) nurse is the person with

whom patients will have the most contact and who will probably be most important to their care.

In hospital it is these specialist nurses who provide 24-hour care, and who monitor and assess an individual's progress. As part of the multi-disciplinary team they will discuss and agree a plan of care and in almost all cases this should be done in consultation with the patient. Although only the psychiatrist and his house officers (junior doctors) have the power to prescribe, the nurse's influence in deciding what to prescribe and in what dosage is very potent.

Modern mental health nurses are skilled practitioners in the field of human activity, with an emphasis on self-awareness, interpersonal and organisational skills. They draw upon social and applied sciences including psychology, sociology, physiology and anatomy, medicine, pharmacology and psychiatry. They may specialise in care areas such as the elderly, rehabilitation, child psychiatry or substance abuse.

A community psychiatric nurse is, as the name suggests, a nurse practitioner who focuses on providing care outside the hospital situation. This focus may be on the prevention of mental distress, the maintenance of existing well-being or the promotion of improved mental health in the community.

Psychiatrist

The psychiatrist is a qualified medical doctor who has gone on to specialise in psychiatry and usually has consultant status. Patients will have very little contact with the consultant psychiatrist, yet as they often appear to have a great deal of power and of course do have certain legal and professional powers that a nurse does not have, will tend to place a great deal of faith in them. They are sometimes disappointed. Indeed, a survey conducted by Mind showed that nurses were the most helpful mental health professional.

While there are many psychiatrists who are sensitive and empathic in the care they provide, many more are neither and see their role as a prescriber of pills.

Some psychiatrists are, however, also trained psychotherapists, understanding the value of a planned programme of care that does not necessarily revolve around medication.

Clinical Psychologist

A clinical psychologist specialises in the assessment and psychological care of mental health problems.

Psychological testing such as for IQ levels or for evidence of deep-seated mental health problems is one area in which they might work. They are also very involved in various therapies such as counselling, family and behaviour therapy.

Mental health social worker

Some social workers choose to specialise in the support of the family of people with mental health problems as well as the social aspects of care of the individual involved.

They can be based in a local mental health centre, mental health hospital or local authority offices. They can provide support and counselling as well as practical advice about welfare rights, local facilities and other day-to-day matters.

Occupational Therapist

An occupational therapist is trained in various methods of helping people maintain and develop many of their social skills. As well as running occupational therapy workshops including carpentry, pottery and craftwork, OTs get involved in reminiscence and group therapy.

Art Therapist

Art therapy works from the basis that a person's fundamental thoughts and feelings are sometimes more easily expressed through images than words. The art therapist allows a client to work with a medium they feel comfortable with and together they can explore what might be happening for the client at that time.

Industrial Therapist

Industrial therapy is designed to help people develop skills and confidence through a working environment. However, while it gives structure to the day and some of the benefits of a working environment, the work is often dull, repetitive and does not earn the patient more than pin money.

Patient involvement in care regimes
Care Plans
For any care regime to stand a chance of success the patient or client must be involved at the earliest opportunity. Under the care programme approach, provision is made for needs assessment and patient involvement and mental health professionals are expected to gain agreement to part or all of any care plan or care programme that is devised.

Mental health care services
Hospital Care
In the UK at present there is a massive change in direction for hospital care for people with mental health problems. In the nineteenth century, well-meaning philanthropists built huge asylums in the countryside where anyone with some form of madness was incarcerated, often for life. By 'mad' it was meant people with a whole range of 'afflictions' such as epilepsy, promiscuous behaviour, hypochondria, melancholia and learning difficulties (sometimes referred to as a mental handicap). As already mentioned, these are now being closed down in favour of treating and supporting people in the community wherever possible with wards on an ordinary district general hospital for people who experience a mental health crisis that needs more intensive care and 24-hour support. Although sometimes criticised as an attempt to save money, this is an important step in breaking down the perceived barriers between the 'well' and the 'ill', the 'sane' and the 'insane', the 'us' and 'them' syndrome. Acute mental health crises are now treated much more like an episode in a person's life rather than an acceptance of a hopeless dependency. Following recovery from the crisis, after-care is offered on a community basis.

Therapeutic Community
In fact this is not really as much a place as a concept and a way of approaching mental health problems from an individual or family point of view.

Secure hospital

A secure hospital or special assessment and supervision service (SASS) unit is a hospital dealing with people who, through some form of mental health problem, have committed a crime and have been imprisoned in places such as Broadmoor or Rampton Hospitals. They are also used for the assessment and care of people with mental health problems who may be particularly prone to aggression. The aim of these units is to rehabilitate people from special prisons into the community.

The multi-disciplinary team

In the more progressive mental health services, the whole emphasis of care is on helping the patient return to the community. Patients are encouraged through a programme of care operated by a team of professionals that will include several or all of the following: a psychiatric nurse, psychiatrist, psychologist, occupational therapist and social worker.

These professionals together make up what is known as a multi-disciplinary team, enabling the patient or client to discuss their problems with people offering different services and who may have input into their care plan (if an in-patient) or care programme (if being discharged). This in theory should lead to better planning and therefore better care. However, the 'ward round', a weekly event held to discuss patients' progress, and/or pre-discharge meeting can in actual fact be an appalling experience for the patient as the poem below, written by someone who was a psychiatric nurse at the time, describes:

Ward round

Engines turning
Pistons churning
Joey's got a hole
in the head.
Psychiatry whirring
constant burning
deep in this house
of the Living Dead.

Magicians weaving
self-righteous preaching
Hum the tune of the
vicar's veil.
Sandra screaming
disbelieving
throw sixpence down
the wishing well.
Pull out the bin
Let's hear her sins
Personal private
tragic Hell.
Joey's in on the
coffin thing a
primary nurse
brought him in.
Draw the curtains
Let's begin
this multi-purpose
Party Din.
I'm choking on the
ego stench
Look at yourselves
what you present.
Damaged bodies
Damaged minds
don't be so bloody
unkind change
this weekly wicked
grind don't be stupid
all the time.
Sandra's laughing
at your lies
Joey sits and hides
his time it won't
be long before
they find that
no-one really has
the time.

Andy Alison

I have attended ward rounds that numbered 12 professionals, including a psychiatrist, two junior doctors, three social workers, two community psychiatric nurses and a psychologist. Into this intimidating environment were brought, individually, several patients who were receiving care at the psychiatric hospital in question. As each patient was brought into the ward round it was impossible to miss the look of horror on their faces as they registered the number of health professionals they had to discuss their pain and personal tragedy in front of. Many health professionals I have spoken to also find ward rounds distressing, some claiming that they cannot look the patient in the eyes. (Whether this is to protect their own or the patient's sensibilities they did not say.) Some psychiatrists and other team members will find other ways of care planning whilst still involving the patient or client, whilst some patients would argue that it is impossible to get to see the psychiatrist at all because they are largely excluded from the planning process. All in all, this is an area of care that still needs to be more openly addressed, particularly given the essential need for good, open communication in providing adequate community care.

Mental health and human rights

Understanding and defending human rights, for ourselves and other people, has been a theme that has dominated the thinking of the twentieth-century Western world. But while there is now perhaps little question about the importance of human rights, there is a greater moral struggle when it comes to deciding the balance between the rights of the individual and the rights of the community, between the rights of the community and the rights of the state, and between the rights of individuals, communities and states.

While much of this book has talked about individual mental well-being from a positive point of view, for some people the lack of their mental well-being may well be caused by severe restrictions of many of their human rights, while for others it can mean that many of their rights are taken away from them – the right to freedom, the right to vote, the right to refuse medication, the right to wear their own clothes. All of these rights can be legally taken from an individual whose mental health state appears to create a risk of their harming themselves or others.

For this reason it is important to understand just what our rights are as individuals, under what circumstances we may have to surrender these rights and, perhaps most crucially, what we can do to protect our rights and the rights of others.

Our rights as individuals are laid down in a number of settings, including the Patients' Charter and the European Commission for Human Rights. Legally enforceable rights are enshrined in law, and in the case of mental well-being, our rights, and the loss of those rights, are laid out in the Mental Health Act 1983.

The Patients' Charter

The Patients' Charter is a set of guidelines that includes both legal and human rights in relation to health care. These state that all persons have a right to:

- Health services appropriate to their needs, regardless of financial means or where they live and without delay. This includes the right to change your hospital doctor if you are unhappy with any aspect of the care you are receiving.
- Be treated with reasonable skill, care and consideration. According to the General Medical Council 'the public are entitled to expect that a registered medical practitioner will afford and maintain a good standard of medical care'. This includes:
    conscientious assessment of the history, symptoms and signs of a patient's condition;
    sufficiently thorough professional attention, examination and, where necessary, diagnostic investigation;
    competent and considerate professional management;
    appropriate and prompt action upon evidence suggesting existence of a condition requiring urgent medical intervention; and
    readiness, where the circumstances warrant it, to consult appropriate professional colleagues.
- Written information about health services, including hospitals, community and general practitioner services.
- Register with a GP with ease and to be able to change without adverse consequences.
- Be informed about all aspects of their condition and proposed care (including the alternatives available), unless they express a wish to the contrary.
- Accept or refuse treatment (including diagnostic procedures) without affecting the standard of alternative care given (under the Mental Health Act 1983 this right has certain restrictions which are outlined below).
- A second opinion.
- The support of a relative or friend at any time.
- Advocacy (*see below*) and interpreting services.
- Choose whether to participate or not in research trials and

be free to withdraw at any time without affecting the standard of alternative care given.

- Only be discharged from hospital after adequate arrangements have been made for their continuing care.
- Privacy for all consultations.
- Be treated at all times with respect for their dignity, personal needs and religious and philosophic beliefs.
- Confidentiality of all records relating to their care.
- Have access to their own health care records (still not a legal right).
- Make a complaint and have it investigated thoroughly, speedily and impartially and be informed of the result.
- An independent investigation into all serious medical or other mishaps whilst in NHS care, whether or not a complaint is made and, where appropriate, adequate redress.

Human rights

The European Commission for Human Rights states that as an individual one should expect to be able to:

- state needs and set priorities independent of role
- be treated with respect as an intelligent, capable and equal human being
- express feelings
- express opinions and values
- say 'yes' or 'no'
- make mistakes
- change one's mind
- say 'I don't understand'
- ask for what one wants
- decline responsibility for other people's problems
- deal with others without being dependent on them for approval
- take full responsibility for one's own actions

The ability to be assertive is seen as important in ensuring individual rights are acknowledged and the following statements are seen as assertive 'rights':

Assertive rights

I have the right to ask for what I want (realising that the other person has a right to say 'no').

I have the right to an opinion, feelings and emotions and to express them appropriately.

I have the right to make statements which have no logical basis and which I do not have to justify.

I have the right to make my own decisions and cope with the consequences.

I have the right to choose whether or not to get involved in the problems of someone else.

I have the right not to know, or to understand, about something.

I have the right to make mistakes.

I have the right to be successful.

I have the right to change my mind.

I have the right to privacy.

I have the right to be alone and independent.

I have the right to change myself and be an assertive person.

Other human rights with regard to mental health care include the right to be listened to, not just at a tribunal, but on a day-to-day basis, the right to be involved in the planning of care and treatment; the right to be involved in the development of mental health service; the right to be treated with dignity regardless of mental state.

As well as Mind, there are many individuals, organisations and self-help groups striving to improve conditions and empower people who receive care via the mental health services. These include:

the consumer movement (consumerism)
patient advocacy
self-advocacy

support groups
mental health services

The Mental Health Act 1983

As mentioned earlier, many of our rights are enshrined in law
and the legislation that should safeguard our rights in relation
to our mental health is called the Mental Health Act 1983. This
Act was brought into being in order to protect individuals and
the community in the event of severe mental distress that
could in some way prove detrimental or dangerous to the
individual suffering the distress or to the public at large.

Attempts have been made to build in safeguards to the Act
to prevent abuse. Second opinions, tribunals and time limits
have all been included in a legal attempt to protect people
who may be very vulnerable and to prevent people being
locked away and forgotten. However, Mind believes there are
still many instances where people are inappropriately
detained in hospital.

The Mental Health Act 1983 is very complicated and
lengthy. There are also issues of interpretation to be considered. For instance, the Mental Health Act states that the Act
applies to people with 'mental illness, arrested or incomplete
development of the mind, psychopathic disorder and any
other disorder or disability of mind'. The term 'mental illness'
is not defined within the Act.

Legal rights under the Mental Health Act 1983

Picture the old black-and-white films, with the evil relative
trying to get some poor soul committed to a lunatic asylum,
usually as part of a plot to get the family wealth or perhaps
run off with a lover. Hopefully those days are over, but there
are without doubt many instances where people who have felt
unable or unwilling to cope with a relative's mental distress
do ask for the relative in question to be committed under the
Mental Health Act. And there are no doubt times when
mental health professionals working in the community feel
they are no longer able to identify and meet the needs of a

person in distress. When the community can no longer cope, compulsory admission to hospital is considered.

Since 1983 and the revision of the Act it is now far more difficult to 'Section' someone. However, it remains very important that people are aware of their rights and the powers of the health professionals. For instance, if you decide that you need the help of mental health professionals and you voluntarily enter a mental health hospital for a period of assessment and possible treatment, then you may well think you have exactly the same rights and considerations as someone entering a general hospital for an operation. This is not the case.

If, after a period of voluntary stay in a mental health hospital, you decide you no longer need help and wish to discharge yourself, and the professionals concerned believe that you are at risk of, say, harming yourself or others, or are not well enough to leave, then they may well decide to keep you in hospital under a Section of the Mental Health Act. They can do this in a number of ways.

In cases where an informal patient who wishes to leave the ward is felt to be at risk of harming themselves or some other person, mental health nurses have the legal right to detain them for up to six hours (Section 5.4: Nurse's holding power). This holding power ceases the minute a doctor steps on to the ward. The doctor may or may not decide to implement a further Section of the Act. However, if a doctor cannot be found (this should be a rare instance) there appears to be nothing within the Act to prevent a nurse implementing a second or even third Section 5.4, thereby in practice preventing a patient from leaving the ward for some considerable period of time.

It is not only patients who have been held on a ward under this Section of the Mental Health Act. In one instance a relative became hostile and abusive whilst visiting a patient on a psychiatric ward and the nurse in charge exercised her powers under the Mental Health Act and held him on the ward under Section 5.4 of the Act. This was, however, an abuse of the nurse's holding power, as a person must be receiving in-patient psychiatric treatment to be held under Section 5.4.

The following parts of the Mental Health Act are also relevant to hospital treatment.

Admission to and discharge from a hospital for people with acute or chronic mental health problems

Informal or voluntary admission (Section 131)

Any person who requires treatment for mental disorder may request informal admission but must be referred by a doctor. In the case of a person under 16 (a minor), this must be on the authority of his parent or guardian. An informal patient is free to leave hospital at any time subject to holding powers or common law powers. In nearly every respect, the legal position of an informal patient is the same as a patient in a general hospital.

Compulsory admission from patient's home (Sections 2, 3 and 4)

Section 2: admission for assessment
Criteria for admission:
- mental disorder which warrants detention in hospital for assessment (treatment may be given)
- detention is necessary for patient's health or safety or for the protection of others

An application for detention under Section 2 of the Mental Health Act (1983) can be made by the individual's nearest relative or an approved social worker. A medical recommendation that the person is detained under this section of the Act must be made by 1) a doctor who knows the patient and 2) an approved medical officer. Two doctors must confirm that:

a) the patient is suffering from mental disorder of a nature or degree which warrants detention in hospital for assessment (or assessment followed by medical treatment) for at least a limited period; and
b) the patient ought to be detained in the interests of their

own health or safety or with a view to the protection of others

Section 2 will terminate after 28 days. Discharge follows:

- termination by the responsible medical officer
- termination by the managers of the hospital
- by the nearest relative (but only with the agreement of the responsible medical officer. If this agreement is not forthcoming then your appeal should be lodged in writing to the hospital managers who can overrule the consultant)
- by a Mental Health Review Tribunal
- by the patient leaving hospital without permission (referred to as absent without leave) until the Section has expired

An appeal against Section 2 must be made within 14 days of admission.

Section 3: admission for treatment
To be brought into hospital under Section 3 of the Mental Health Act (1983) a person has to be suffering from one of four legal classifications of mental disorder:

- mental illness
- severe mental impairment
- mental impairment
- psychopathic disorder

In the case of psychopathic disorder or mental impairment, treatment must be likely to alleviate or prevent deterioration in patient condition (in many instances psychopathic/sociopathic disorders do not respond to treatment).

In instances where the possibility exists that a person may be a danger to themselves or others they can be detained under Section 3 of the Mental Health Act.

Like Section 2, application to have someone brought into hospital under Section 3 can be made by the nearest relative or an approved social worker. However, the social worker cannot make the application without the consent of the nearest relative.

Again, like Section 2, medical recommendation must be sought from a doctor who knows the patient plus one other approved medical officer.

One doctor must confirm that:

a) the patient is suffering from one of the four specified categories of mental disorder of a nature or degree which makes it appropriate for them to receive medical treatment in hospital; and
b) if a patient is suffering from a psychopathic disorder or mental impairment, such treatment is likely to 'alleviate or prevent a deterioration' of their condition; and
c) it is necessary for their own health or safety or for the protection of others that they receive such treatment and it cannot be provided unless he is detained under this Section.

A person can be kept in hospital for six months under Section 3 of the Mental Health Act, and this can be renewed for a further six months after this, followed by periods of one year. Section 3 can be terminated by the responsible medical officer, the hospital managers, the nearest relative (again, like Section 2, a request for termination can be overruled by the responsible medical officer) and the Mental Health Review Tribunal.

If a person goes absent without leave for 28 days (Section 18 (4)) or for six months (Section 17 (5)), the Section automatically becomes terminated.

Section 4: admission for assessment in an emergency
The criteria for admission under Section 4 of the Mental Health Act 1983 is the same as that for Section 2, when admission is of urgent necessity. Application can be made by the nearest relative or approved social worker although Section 4 only needs the recommendation of the doctor who knows the patient.

Section 4 will expire after 72 hours unless a second medical recommendation is received.

It can be terminated by the responsible medical officer or by the hospital managers or if the patient goes absent without leave until the Section expires.

Section 4 of the Mental Health Act 1983 cannot be appealed against.

Sections 5.2 and 5.4

It is important that people entering hospital as informal or voluntary patients are aware that if they wish to leave and their leaving is believed to be inadvisable by medical or nursing staff, then they can be legally detained.

A doctor can hold a patient in hospital pending an application for compulsory detention for 72 hours. This can be terminated by the responsible medical officer or hospital managers.

It is also possible for a patient to be detained in hospital for a maximum of six hours by nursing staff, if they believe that prevention from leaving hospital is necessary for the protection of the patient or others and it is not possible to gain the immediate attendance of the responsible medical officer or nominated substitute.

Guardianship (Sections 7–10)

A guardianship order is usually pursued where the patient or client is felt to be particularly vulnerable to exploitation.

A guardianship order lasts for six months, is renewable for a further six months and then for one year at a time.

A guardianship order can be applied for by an approved social worker or the nearest relative.

In order to impose a guardianship order, two doctors must confirm:

a) a patient is suffering from one of the four specified categories of mental disorder of a nature or degree which warrants reception into guardianship; and
b) it is necessary in the interests of the patient's welfare or for the protection of others.

The patient must be over 16 to be considered for guardianship and the guardian must be a local social service authority or person approved by the same.

Under Section 8, the guardian has the following powers:

- to require the patient to live at a place specified by the guardian

- to require the patient to attend places specified by the guardian for occupation, training or medical treatment (although the guardian cannot force the patient to undergo treatment)
- to ensure that a doctor, social worker or other person specified by the guardian can see the patient at home

Discharge from guardianship is by the responsible medical officer, local social services authority, the nearest relative or a Mental Health Review Tribunal.

Note: Supervised discharge (Section 25) is a new concept that builds upon guardianship and includes something called the 'power to convey'. The power to convey means that the nominated supervisor (agreed on discharge from hospital) has the legal power to take the patient to an agreed place. This power can be delegated to a third party, such as the police. At the time of writing it is too early to assess the implications of supervised discharge in practice, although mental health professionals and service users alike have expressed many reservations.

Section 136: mentally disordered persons found in public places

If it appears to a police officer that a person in a public place is 'suffering from mental disorder' and is 'in immediate need of care or control', he can take that person to a 'place of safety', usually a hospital. Section 136 lasts for a maximum of 72 hours, so that a person can be examined by a doctor and interviewed by an approved social worker and 'any necessary arrangements' made for their treatment or care.

Section 135: warrant to search for and remove patients

If there is reasonable cause to suspect that a person is suffering from mental disorder and:

a) is being ill-treated or neglected or not kept under proper control; or
b) is unable to care for himself and lives alone

then a magistrate issues a warrant authorising a police officer (with a doctor and a search warrant) to enter any premises where a person is believed to be and remove him to a place of safety (*see also* supervised discharge).

Patients involved in criminal proceedings (Part III)

Hospital order (Section 37)

Section 37 lasts for six months, is renewable for a further six months and then for one year at a time.

A hospital order can be made by Crown court or magistrates' court in the case of an offender convicted of an offence which it could punish with a prison sentence (such offences include manslaughter but not murder). A magistrates' court can make a hospital order without recording a conviction if the offender is suffering from mental illness or severe mental impairment, and magistrates are satisfied that they committed the act with which they are charged.

The court can make the hospital order on evidence from two doctors that:

a) the offender is suffering from one of the four specified categories of mental disorder of a nature or degree which makes detention for medical treatment appropriate and
b) if the patient is suffering from psychopathic disorder or mental impairment, such treatment is likely to 'alleviate or prevent a deterioration' of their condition; and
c) taking into account all the relevant circumstances, including past history and character of the offender and alternative methods of dealing with them, a hospital order is the most suitable option.

Discharge from a hospital order is by a responsible medical officer, hospital managers or a Mental Health Review Tribunal.

Section 41: restriction order

The length of time a restriction order runs for is decided by a court or is without limit. It is only used for people who are perceived as being very dangerous.

The Crown court which made the hospital order under

Section 37 can also impose a restriction order if:

a) this is necessary to protect the public from 'serious harm'; and
b) at least one of the doctors who made recommendations for the hospital order gave their evidence orally.

Magistrates' courts cannot make a restriction order but can commit an offender to a Crown court so that a Section 41 can be imposed.

Discharge from a restriction order is either by the Home Secretary or by application to the Mental Health Review Tribunal.

Section 47: transfer to hospital from prison

Section 47 runs provisionally for six months, is renewable for a further six months and then for one year at a time. If the Home Secretary imposes a restriction direction (Section 49), it continues in force until the earliest date on which the patient would have been released from prison with remission.

The procedure for a Section 47 is that the Home Secretary orders the transfer if satisfied by evidence from two doctors that:

a) the offender is suffering from one of the four specified categories of mental disorder of a nature or degree which makes detention for medical treatment appropriate; and
b) if the patient is suffering from psychopathic disorder or mental impairment, such treatment is likely to 'alleviate or prevent a deterioration' of their condition.

If no restriction direction has been imposed, the patient can be discharged by the responsible medical officer, hospital managers or a Mental Health Review Tribunal, which can only recommend discharge to the Home Secretary.

Other powers of the courts

Section 35: remand to hospital for medical report

The Crown court or magistrates' court can remand an accused person to hospital for up to 28 days, renewable for further periods of 28 days to a maximum of 12 weeks in all, on evidence from one doctor that:

a) there is 'reason to suspect' that the person is suffering from one of the four specified categories of mental disorder; and
b) it would be 'impracticable' for a report on their mental condition to be made if they were remanded on bail.

Section 36: remand to hospital for treatment

A Crown court can remand an accused person to hospital for treatment for up to 28 days, renewable for further periods of 28 days to a maximum of 12 weeks in all, on evidence from two doctors that they are suffering from mental illness or severe mental impairment of a nature or degree which makes detention for treatment appropriate.

Section 38: interim hospital order

A Crown court or magistrates' court can make an interim hospital order of 12 weeks, renewable for 28 days at a time to a maximum of six months, on evidence from two doctors that:

a) a convicted offender is suffering from one of the four specified categories of mental disorder; and
b) there is reason to suppose that it is appropriate for the order to be made.

A hospital order or prison sentence may subsequently be passed for an offender who has been subject to an interim hospital order.

Supervision registers

In 1994, the government asked for the setting up of registers which held the name and details of persons in contact with the psychiatric services who were deemed to be 'at risk', either to others, from others or of self-neglect. The use of supervision registers was seen as highly questionable and possibly illegal. Where supervision registers operate (not all health trusts have implemented them, some preferring to use the care programme approach effectively) patients should be informed if their name is recorded and the reasons for this discussed.

Consent to treatment

The Mental Health Act contains the legal situation with regard to a patients' right to refuse treatment. It applies to any patient detained under the Act except those detained under Section 4 *(see above)*, Section 5 *(see above)*, Section 35 *(see above)*, patients conditionally discharged under Sections 42, 73 or 74 who have not been brought back into hospital, as well as Section 135 *(see above)* and Section 136 *(see above)*.

Surgical operations that interfere with the workings of the brain (e.g. lobotomy) are dealt with under Section 57 of the Act. In this instance it is necessary for the patient themselves to give consent and for a registered medical practitioner plus two other people who are not registered medical practitioners to state in writing that the person to undergo the operation is capable of understanding the nature, purpose and likely effects of the operation and that they have given their consent.

However, very few people coming into contact with the mental health services will have any dealings with Section 57, as operations to remove parts of the brain are rare, and it is more likely to be in the area of refusing medication or ECT that the patients' rights might well be dismissed.

Refusing medication: the informal patient

It is a sad fact that many doctors and nurses working within the mental health field do not listen to what patients have to say about their medication. Indeed, all too often any concerns raised by the patient about medication are regarded as 'inappropriate behaviour' and refusal to take medication is regarded as 'non-compliance'. Non-compliance in turn can have unpleasant consequences for the patient, including being evidence for detaining an informal patient, and in the case of the detained patient it may result in evidence against the termination of a section and quite possibly medication given by injection (most medication is given orally) against the patient's wishes.

As the law stands at present, an informal patient in a mental health hospital has the same rights as a patient in hospital with a physical illness:

- The implications of the treatment or procedure should be explained (in the case of psychotropic drugs or ECT, this should include an explanation about side-effects).
- The patient retains the right to refuse the treatment offered.

Treatment given without consent is regarded as battery, a form of trespass to the person, and this can lead to legal action in the criminal and civil courts.

In the case of what is seen as 'urgent necessity' a doctor might decide, following consultation with colleagues, to give treatment where informed consent is uncertain and the patient is at risk. This authority is derived from common law.

A relative's consent has no validity under the law.

Refusing medication: the detained patient

The nature of some mental health problems can mean that the sufferer is not aware of the nature and extent of what they are experiencing and the possible consequences to themselves and others. For instance a person who is experiencing an extreme manic episode may well not eat or sleep for days and be in danger of putting such a strain on their physical system that they may collapse and die from exhaustion. However, because they are so elated in mood they may well respond to the offer of treatment by saying that they have never felt so well in their lives. Their insight may well be impaired, perhaps partially, perhaps totally. In such instances it may be necessary to give treatment to get the person to a state whereby they can discuss their care with nursing staff or their doctor. Where medication has to be given without consent, specific statutory authority may be required.

There has been for many years fierce debate over who should decide the need to give treatment without consent. However, although the legislators have done their best to build in safeguards for the patient by bringing in second opinions, it can do nothing to prevent clinicians persuading these so-called 'independent opinions' to see their point of view. I witnessed an occupational therapist support the decision to give ECT to a patient who was unable to give consent despite the fact that she admitted that she did not really know the patient and had indeed only seen her in passing on a couple of occasions. Despite the fact that the occupational therapist made her reluctance known, she was persuaded to support the proposed treatment.

The mental health consumer movement

Traditionally, receivers or purchasers of goods and services have been fairly powerless and often vulnerable to unscrupulous providers and profiteers. The need to protect consumers and also to instil a stronger sense of morality and responsibility in providers resulted in the growth of the consumer movement. Listening to the customer became a watchword for successful organisations and market research, the communication link between goods and service providers and their customers.

This movement was initially slow to catch on in the UK, but over the last ten years under a confident Tory government, consumerism has encompassed not only commerce and industry but the public health care sector as well.

The NHS, during the greater part of the 1980s, was the focus of attention for customer satisfaction surveys. Usually instigated by senior management, these surveys were developed and carried out as a way of improving the quality of care that patients received. Concentrating mainly on the so-called 'hotel services' (quality of food, comfort, pleasantness of environment), it neatly skirted issues of relevance to user empowerment, such as involvement in treatment and access to medical records, and rarely looked to users of mental health services, preferring to tap into the feelings of satisfaction or otherwise experienced by people using the acute general services (e.g. maternity, medical and surgical wards).

As a form of promoting mental health rights, consumerism does not show any great promise, except perhaps where it stimulates mental health workers to see patients as partners in a giving and receiving relationship (the giving and receiving goes both ways, not just from professional to patient).

Patients' councils

A patients' council is a meeting of hospital residents or

patients without the presence of staff (which differs from community meetings, where staff and patients meet together). The first one was established in Nottingham. The meeting does not need a statutory number of patients to attend and attendance is from choice. Any issues of importance to patients can be discussed and decisions made about how to improve the quality of the environment, the care received or anything else of importance to the patients themselves.

In Nottingham the patients' councils from individual wards elected representatives (always a patient) to meet other patient representatives of other wards at a hospital council to discuss matters that affected all wards in order to take these issues to hospital management.

The role of advocacy in achieving mental health rights

The term 'advocacy' means the pleading of a case on behalf of another. The main kinds of advocacy that exist in the mental health field are:

   patient or citizen advocacy
   paid advocacy
   self-advocacy

Patient or citizen advocacy

This is a form of lay advocacy or representation. The lay advocate is an independent, unpaid and valued person who has a special one-to-one relationship with a service user and represents their interests.

Paid advocacy

This is usually a professional representative such as a solicitor.

Self-advocacy

Speaking up for ourselves is all too rarely encouraged, particularly if what we have to say goes against the grain.

And so in many areas of our lives we tend to allow or even pay for others to speak on our behalf – lawyers, trade union representatives and politicians are just a few of the people who may represent our views and feelings on a variety of issues. However, the problem with representatives is that quite often they may think they know how we feel and what we want but in actual fact may be quite out of touch. They may not consult fully enough with us or they may think they know better. For this reason it is often important that we do speak up for ourselves. To do this effectively we need knowledge, skill and support. And perhaps courage.

For people who have used mental health services, speaking up for themselves is far from easy. They are told, and often accept, that doctor and nurse know best. They are pushed into a passive, accepting role, and any attempt to reject this role is often seen as a symptom of a psychiatric illness rather than a welcome sign of well-being. Given the amount of social stigma that is attached to mental health problems of most kinds, it is a very brave person who stands up and admits their situation, let alone fights for their needs. It is, for many people, far less painful to put their experience behind them and to get on with their lives.

However, despite the very real difficulties and risks of self-advocacy, there are those who do wish to make their views known and implement change and they draw strength from linking up with like-minded others.

Survivors Speak Out (*see* Useful Addresses) is a national mental health service users' self-advocacy network that facilitates:

- communication between individuals and groups involved in self-advocacy
- consciousness-raising for survivors and mental health workers
- information for mental health workers about the value of self-advocacy and opportunities for them to give their personal and financial support

This network does not represent users of mental health services but works to help them represent themselves, and to encourage service providers to listen and promulgate self-advocacy amongst patients.

The role of professionals

Mental health professionals come in for a great deal of criticism when it comes to patients' rights, some justified, some not.

Obviously mental health professionals have a legal obligation to protect individuals from themselves and communities from individuals. There are instances where nursing staff have to deal with people who, because of their desperate mental state, will go to quite extraordinary lengths to harm themselves, even to take their own lives. And while it might be quite possible to accept that everyone has the right to take their own life if they so choose, in a rational state of mind, mental health nurses often have to deal with people who, when they are well, would not wish to harm themselves or die, but whose mental distress might well include a strong desire to self-harm. It is the responsibility of mental health professionals to get people over this stage and to a point where they can make clear choices for themselves.

The Mental Health Act Commission

The Mental Health Act Commission is a special health authority authorised to keep under review all aspects of the care of patients detained under the Mental Health Act 1983. It can investigate complaints, appoint panels to give a second opinion on consent to treatment and draw up codes of practice for mental health workers. It comprises approximately 90 part-time commissioners, drawn mainly from the professions involved in the mental health services.

7

Drug treatments

The psychiatrist I saw on the NHS told me that I was suffering from depression and immediately prescribed anti-depressants. The emphasis seemed to be on getting me 'back to normal' as he put it – never mind the fact that I was actually desperate to change my life and didn't want to go back to just passively accepting things.

This chapter looks at the use and possible abuse of psychotropic drugs prescribed in an attempt to help those suffering from mental health problems, also the damaging effects of long-term drug use.

The need for drugs

In the same way that drawing an analogy between physical and mental illness does not in the long run aid understanding, so it goes for chemotherapy, or drug treatments for mental health problems. Patients with a physical illness will in most instances start to feel better shortly after medication and will be grateful to the medical practitioner for prescribing the treatment. Patients with a mental illness may not welcome the drug treatment and it may even, at times, make them feel worse.

Take for example someone whose mental distress makes them believe, temporarily, that people are trying to kill them. Prescribed medication may be seen as a poison and therefore may be refused. The medication is designed to tackle the more distressing symptoms of the illness. But someone who is suffering from a psychotic disorder will be unaware that the symptoms are just that, because they will be unable to distinguish reality from fantasy. For these people their experience of the drug, certainly initially, may well focus on the side-effects they experience.

And yet while few of us would have any qualms about a concoction of heroin and morphine being administered to prevent agonising pain in a patient terminally ill with cancer, most of us would react with horror at the thought of someone taking the same drugs to dull some emotional pain, or even just for kicks. While some of our horror stems from fear, ignorance and prejudice, our more rational side is concerned about possible addiction and damage to the body. And yet prescribed psychotropic drugs for mental health problems can have both of these side-effects. The difference is that someone somewhere will make a decision that the distress associated with possible long-term damage is outweighed by the distress caused by the mental health problem. This person is usually a doctor and, all too often, the patient passively accepts the prescription. What happens less frequently is an honest discussion about some of the unwanted side-effects of the medication. Doctors often justify this by saying that the patient would only be anxious if they knew in advance what the unpleasant side-effects might be, and might even refuse to take the medication. However, how much more anxiety and distress does it cause when the person taking the medication then experiences the unpleasant effects, whilst expecting to feel better or well? It certainly is not justified in any circumstances to keep information on the side-effects of drugs from patients. People have a right to information and this position is central to Mind policy. A person may well be willing and able to tolerate any initial unpleasantness from a drug, or work with the doctor to minimise it, in order to gain the longer-term benefit. However, in order to do this, clinicians, whether doctors or nurses, need to engage the patient in an open and honest discussion about their treatment. Information is essential.

Information about drug treatment can also involve a person much more closely in their care and treatment, helping them to feel more empowered, more in control and therefore much more likely to benefit from it. Helping people to make informed choices about drug treatments, discussing why one anti-depressant might be more useful than another, encouraging the person to talk about the experience of the drug and admitting another treatment might be more useful, together with regular reviews of the effectiveness of the drug, perhaps by self-assessment, would limit over-prescription and ineffective prescription.

Drugs and their side-effects

Major tranquillisers

Name	Proprietary name	Side-effects
Clopenthixol	**Clopixol**	restlessness
Chlorpromazine	**Largactyl**	tremor
Chlorprothixene	**Taractan**	stiffness
Droperidon	**Droleptan**	loss of facial expression
Flupenthixol	**Depixol**	dry mouth
Haloperidol	**Haldol**	blurred vision
	Serenace	constipation
Oxypertine	**Integrin**	difficulty in passing water
Pericyazine	**Neulactil**	increased appetite
Perphenazine	**Fentazin**	faintness on suddenly standing up
Pimozide	**Orap**	sensitivity of skin to sunlight
Prochloroperazine	**Stemetil**	lowering of body temperature
	Vertigon spansules	
Promazine	**Sparine**	odd movements of body and face
Sulpiridine	**Dolmatil**	increases the effect of alcohol
Thiopropazate	**Dartalan**	
Trifluoroperazine	**Stelazine**	
Trifluperidon	**Triperidol**	

The above side-effects can vary in extent depending on which drug is used and the individual person. The unpleasant effects can often be temporary.

Major tranquillisers

(given by injection)

Name	Proprietary name
Clopenthixol	**Clopixol**
Flupenthixol decanoate	**Depixol**
Fluphenazine decanoate	**Modecate**
Fluphenazine enanthate	**Moditen**
Fluspirilene	**Redeptin**
Haloperidol decanoate	
Haldol decanoate	
Pipothiazine palmitate	
Piportil depot	

Long-term use of neuroleptic drugs, particularly phenothiazines, can cause permanent side-effects:

● *acute distonic reactions*
   The symptoms of an acute distonic reaction are the sudden onset of retrocollis, torticollis, facial grimaces or distortions, dysarthria, difficult or laboured breathing and uncontrollable muscle movements or spasms. This type of reaction needs to be countered by further drug treatment in the form of an anti-Parkinson drug such as Procyclidine (Kemadrin), Benzotropine (Cogentin), Biperiden (Akineton) or Orphenadrine (Disipal).

● *akithisia*
   Agitation or 'motor restlessness' shows itself as an inability to relax. Again, this side-effect is countered by another drug such as Diazepam.

● *tardive dyskinesia*
   This extremely distressing condition can occur after prolonged treatment with anti-psychotic drugs and might be exacerbated by stress. Symptoms are most likely to be manifest in the face but can also appear in the arms and legs. They include involuntary movements such as spasms, twitches, grasping movements, lip-sucking and jaw grating.

- *Parkinson-like condition*
  Because anti-psychotic drugs act by blocking dopamine receptors, this results in a build-up of dopamine as the brain tries to get this neurotransmitter to get through. This causes a similar response in the body to that of Parkinson's disease. The symptoms are a physical rigidity, akinesia and tremor.

- *circulatory problems*

Tricyclic anti-depressants

Name	Proprietary name	Common side-effects
Amitriptyline	**Tryptizol**	
Domical		
Elavil		
Lentizol (S-R)		
	Saroten	
Butryptyline	**Evadyne**	
Clomipramine	**Anafranil**	blurred vision
Desipramine	**Pertofran**	constipation
Dibenzepin	**Noveril**	difficulty in passing water
Dothiepin	**Prothiaden**	dry mouth
Doxepin	**Sinequan**	confusion in the elderly
Imipramine	**Tofranil**	increase in effect of alcohol
	Berkomine	
	Praminil	can aggravate symptoms in those with schizophrenia
Iprindole	**Prondol**	
Lofepramine	**Gamanil**	weight gain
Maprotiline	**Ludiomil**	
Mianserin	**Bolvidon**	
	Norval	
Nomifensine	**Merital**	
Nortriptyline	**Allegron**	
	Aventyl	
Protriptyline	**Concordin**	
Trazodone	**Molipaxin**	

Name	Proprietary name
Trimipramine	**Surmontil**
Viloxazine	**Vivalan**
Fluvoxamine	**Faverin**

MAOI anti-depressants

Name	Proprietary name	Common side-effects
Iproniazid	**Marsilid**	faintness on suddenly standing up
Isocarboxazid	**Marplan**	
Phenelzine	**Nardil**	dangerous interactions with some other drugs
Tranylcypromine	**Parnate**	dangerous interactions with some foods (*see below*) and increase in the effect of alcohol

Food to avoid when taking MAOIs (Monamine Oxidase Inhibitors):
Any form of cheese, especially cream cheese, meat and yeast extracts such as Bovril, Marmite and Oxo, broad beans, avocado pears, pickled herrings, food which might be 'going off'. Proprietary cough and cold medicines should be avoided. Chocolate, yoghurt, cream and game can also, on occasions, cause a reaction.

Minor tranquillisers

Name	Proprietary name	Common side-effects
Triazolam	**Halcion**	
Alprazolam	**Xanax**	
Bromazepam	**Lexotan**	
Fluitrazepam	**Rohypnol**	
Lorazepam	**Almazine** **Ativan**	
Lormetazepam	**Noctamid**	
Oxazepam	**Serenid-D**	

Name	Proprietary name	Common side-effects
Temazepam	**Euhypnos** **Normison**	
Chlordiazepoxide	**Librium**	drowsiness
Clobazepam	**Frisium**	confusion
Clorazepate	**Tranxene**	impaired performance on tasks like driving and working machinery
Diazepam	**Alupram** **Atensine** **Evacalm**	
Solis		
	Stesolid	
Valium	**Roche**	
Valrelease		
Flurazepam	**Dalmane**	
Ketazolam	**Anxon**	
Medazepam	**Nobrium**	
Nitrazepam	**Mogadon** **Nitrodos** **Sommite** **Surem** **Unisomnia**	
Parazepam	**Centrax**	

Lithium treatment and its side-effects

Lithium is a salt that is naturally present in our bodies, and lithium carbonate is given to people who suffer from manic depression while they are relatively stable in an attempt to maintain a biochemical stability. Lithium levels in the body have to be monitored closely as too high a level can be extremely toxic. Side-effects include nausea, diarrhoea and a metallic taste in the mouth. Feeling shaky, consuming more water than normal as well as passing a greater amount of urine are matters of concern and should be reported to a doctor as soon as possible. Failure to act upon these signals, which may be a warning of toxicity, could result in damage to the kidneys.

Electroplexy

Electroplexy, ECT, electro-convulsive therapy – these are all names given to one of the most controversial forms of treatment available for mental health problems of a severe depressive nature.

ECT is carried out under anaesthetic with the use of a muscle relaxant by placing electrodes on either temple (bi-lateral approach) or on one temple and forehead (unilateral approach) and passing a small electric current across the brain for approximately four seconds. This electric 'shock' induces a short epileptic fit. The muscle relaxant reduces the physical proportions of the fit, thereby limiting the amount of physical damage a patient might otherwise sustain.

Although it is not known how electroplexy works and it is by no means effective in many cases, around 20,000 people have ECT every year, some 2,000 receiving this treatment compulsorily. Forty three per cent of the people in the Experiencing Psychiatry survey who had had ECT reported it as being helpful, whilst 37 per cent reported it as being unhelpful.

Trials comparing real and simulated ECT found that while those receiving the real ECT showed an improvement in symptoms sooner than those who did not receive it, there appeared to be no appreciable difference two weeks later.

Although the muscle relaxant minimises the convulsion or fit that the patient experiences and the anaesthetic means that they have no memory of the treatment, patients can find the anticipation of ECT and the after-effects (memory loss, headaches) extremely distressing. ECT can also be quite distressing to watch, regardless of the measures taken to minimise the distress to the patient.

Psychiatry recognises the following risks of ECT: '. . . each application inevitably leads to a variable period of drowsi-ness, confusion and anterograde amnesia [forgetting new information], commonly causes headache and nausea, and may lead to the occasional loss of personal memories.'

Whilst there are patients who report, and clinicians who have witnessed, very rapid elevations in mood and function-ing following ECT, there is some feeling that it is the damage it causes – 'amnesia, denial, euphoria, apathy, wide and unpredictable mood swings, helplessness and submissiveness' – which is the reason behind this. However, regardless of the short-term outcome, it is the longer-term outcome that is perhaps the proof of the pudding. Do people go on to work out their underlying difficulties and avoid repeated bouts of severe depression? Or is ECT a short-term treatment with possible damaging long-term consequences? This area is acknowledged as being under-researched.

Agreeing to ECT

Patient consent or a second opinion is necessary before treatment can be given. However, patients and their relatives need to be aware of how this consent can sometimes be obtained (see Chapter 6).

Situations whereby ECT is used as a punishment, as shown in *One Flew Over the Cuckoo's Nest*, are now hopefully rare, although health professionals' frustration over the slow progress made by some patients can make recourse to ECT more likely.

Perhaps in an ideal world we would need little or no recourse to drugs. However, the world we live in is far from ideal, and it is often those who suffer most from it who experience mental health problems. At present, drug treatment retains a significant role in the care of mental distress.

8

Alternative treatments

While drugs are important for the self-management of mental
health problems, there are alternatives as well as complementary treatments.

Many alternative treatments are associated with physical
ailments. However, as it is not really possible to segregate the
mind and body, even the physical treatments can be very
therapeutic and if not holistic themselves (as some are) they
can be used as part of a holistic approach to mental well-
being. So, although in some cases the distinction is arbitrary
and can be argued, physical therapies are included here.

It is only possible here to give a brief description of the
alternatives to orthodox drug treatment and what mental
health problems they might help with, but there are many
books available from libraries and bookshops that give much
greater detail. The Resources section at the end of the book
may also prove helpful.

Acupuncture

> What is acupuncture? It's concerned for the mental-emo-
> tional states of people; very much concerned with nutrition.
> It uses in its therapeutics not only needles, but also finger
> pressure. It uses heat in the form of moxibustion. Nowa-
> days, they are using laser beams and ultrasonics, and some
> people inject homoeopathic remedies into acupuncture
> points. So there are all sorts of ways of dealing with the
> energy – Chi energy.
>
> Joe Goodman, Ex-President of the British Acupuncture Association

Mainly associated with alleviating pain, acupuncture has also been used as part of a holistic approach to some addictions such as drinking or smoking. The patient's co-operation and will-power are essential for successful treatment.

For people who really cannot stand the thought of the needles, acupressure, which works by locating key points in relation to the pain or disorder and applying pressure, is an option (*see also* Shiatsu).

Aikido

Aikido is a form of self-defence. Non-aggressive and non-violent, it uses body movements to deflect an attacker's aggressive force. This form of martial art does not require physical strength and is suitable for people of most ages. It exercises all parts of the body, developing flexibility, co-ordination, balance and quick reactions. It teaches that there is no real separation between body and mind, and provides an important emotional and spiritual discipline.

Alexander technique

Although the Alexander technique is concerned primarily with posture, its creator, F. Matthias Alexander, was not concerned just with physiological (bodily) improvements but with 'the restoration and maintenance of psycho-physical efficiency and conditions of well-being'. Correct posture can help with tiredness and listlessness as well as preventing headaches.

Anthroposophical medicine

Based on the philosophy and teachings of Rudolph Steiner, anthroposophy should be interpreted to mean 'awareness of one's humanity'. Awareness of one's self (posture, gestures, etc.), self-expression through music, hydrotherapy, art therapy, all these and more may well be employed by an anthroposophical doctor (who should always be a qualified orthodox doctor who has undertaken a post-graduate course in anthroposophical medicine).

This approach is very much to do with lifestyle rather than taking medication for ailments.

Applied kinesiology

Sometimes known as 'touch for health', applied kinesiology is based on special muscle testing techniques which enable weaknesses to be detected and corrections to be made through touching and positioning. Correcting these weaknesses allows the body's energies to flow unhampered.

This physical therapy is good for tackling physical tensions and preventing pain and discomfort. Applied kinesiology has achieved much success in the treatment of allergies, in particular food allergies.

Aromatherapy

Aromatherapy involves the use of oils made from essences of plants. These essential oils are massaged into the skin, inhaled or used in bathing. Aromatherapists have successfully treated people suffering from depression, even long-term depression that has not responded to other types of treatment, both orthodox and non-orthodox. In fact it has been suggested that almost any disorder that might be classified as psychosomatic or stress-related may be successfully treated through aromatherapy.

Art therapy

Art therapy is used as a vehicle for expression, particularly in situations where it may be difficult to express thoughts and feelings vocally.

Art was originally a form of occupational therapy, then it was realised by psychoanalysts that drawings and paintings expressed what was going on in people's minds.

While art therapy can be used to help individuals understand themselves, it can also be useful for the off-loading of powerful emotions such as anger.

It has been used successfully in the treatment of mental health problems such as anorexia nervosa as well as addiction to alcohol and drugs.

Assertiveness training

Difficulty in asserting your rights, opinions and beliefs undermines your ability to take care of yourself, resulting in low self-esteem and poor self-worth. These in turn make it very difficult to assert yourself, as you do not believe your rights, opinions and beliefs have value, or as much value as those of others. Assertiveness training can be very useful for helping you to refuse unwelcome demands, to set boundaries in relationships and to deal with emotions such as anger, and are often available through adult education evening and day classes.

Autogenic training

Autogenic (meaning 'generated from within') training involves clients learning to put themselves into an auto-hypnotic state through imagining sensations of warmth and heaviness in their limbs.

It is very effective in relieving stress disorders and promoting relaxation, and can also be used to change attitudes and behaviour by making positive statements to yourself when in a deeply relaxed state.

Although the techniques can be learned from a book, it is better to attend a course of sessions with an experienced and trained autogenic worker, as the techniques can sometimes provoke powerful reactions.

Bach flower remedies

You will be most unlikely to find these offered as an alternative for mental distress in any hospital, whether NHS or private, yet the Bach system and remedies were discovered and developed by a doctor who had been a Harley Street consultant, bacteriologist and homoeopath for over 20 years – pretty impeccable references.

The late Edward Bach, MB, BS, MRCS, LRCP, DPH gave up a very successful practice in 1930 to work on developing remedies from the plant world which could be used to restore vitality to the sick. He was particularly interested in people who had both some physical ailment and the negative thought processes that accompany illness. He believed that tackling the negative thinking would enable the sufferer to use their mental energies to assist their healing.

He discovered, in a spiritual rather than scientific manner, 38 flowers that had a positive effect upon different negative states of mind. These were:

Agrimony:	Those who hide worries behind a brave face
Aspen:	Apprehension for no known reason
Beech:	Critical and intolerant of others
Centaury:	Weak willed, exploited or imposed upon
Cerato:	Those who doubt their own judgement, seek confirmation from others
Cherry Plum:	Uncontrolled, irrational thoughts
Chestnut Bud:	Refuses to learn by experience, continually repeats the same mistakes
Chicory:	Over-possessive (self-centred, clinging and over-protective, especially of loved ones)
Clematis:	Inattentive, dreamy, absent-minded, mental escapism
Crab Apple:	The 'Cleanser'. Self-disgust/detestation. Ashamed of ailments
Elm:	Overwhelmed; inadequacy and responsibility
Gentian:	Despondency
Gorse:	Pessimism, defeatism – 'Oh, what's the use!'
Heather:	Talkative (obsessed with own troubles and experiences)
Holly:	Hatred, envy, jealousy, suspicion
Honeysuckle:	Living in the past, nostalgic; home-sickness
Hornbeam:	'Monday morning' feeling, procrastination
Impatiens:	Impatience, irritability
Larch:	Lack of self-confidence, feeling inferior, fearing failure

Mimulus:	Fear of known things. Shyness, timidity
Mustard:	'Dark cloud' that descends, making one saddened and low for no known reason
Oak:	Normally strong/courageous, but no longer able to struggle bravely against illness and/or adversity
Olive:	Fatigued, drained of energy
Pine:	Guilt complex, blames self even for mistakes of others. Always apologising
Red Chestnut:	Obsessed by care and concern for others
Rock Rose:	Suddenly alarmed, scared, panicky
Rock Water:	Rigid-minded, self-denying
Scleranthus:	Uncertainty/indecision/vacillation. Fluctuating moods
Star of Bethlehem:	For all the effects of serious news, or fright following an accident, etc.
Sweet Chestnut:	Utter dejection, bleak outlook
Vervain:	Over-enthusiasm, fanatical beliefs
Vine:	Dominating/inflexible/tyrannical/autocratic/arrogant.
Walnut:	Assists in adjustment to transition or change, e.g. puberty, menopause, divorce, new surroundings
Water Violet:	Proud, reserved, enjoys being alone
White Chestnut:	Persistent unwanted thoughts. Preoccupation with some worry or episode. Mental arguments
Wild Oats:	Helps determine one's intended path in life
Wild Rose:	Resignation, apathy
Willow:	Resentment, embitterment, 'poor me'
Rescue Remedy:	A combination of Cherry Plum, Clematis, Impatiens, Rock Rose, Star of Bethlehem. All-purpose emergency composite for effects of anguish, examinations, going to the dentist, etc. Comforting, calming and reassuring to those distressed by startling experiences

From a leaflet distributed by the Bach Centre

For a deeper understanding and explanation, important to successful use of the Remedies, there are many books on the subject. Dr Bach's original descriptions are in his book *Twelve Healers*.

Biofeedback

Biofeedback is a process which relies on electronic machines to give information on physiological processes such as heart rate, blood pressure, temperature, muscle tension and brain-wave activity. A person using biofeedback can change their thoughts and behaviour to bring about a desired result, such as lessening tension. This reduction in tension is in turn fed back to the person by the machine.

Biofeedback is used in conjunction with forms of relaxation mentioned elsewhere in this chapter, such as autogenic training, meditation and breathing exercises, and has been shown to be useful in treating stress-related conditions such as high blood pressure, tension headaches and sleep problems.

Chiropractic

Chiropractors, like osteopaths, treat conditions such as backache, sciatica, neck, shoulder and arm pain and headaches. They specialise in the diagnosis and treatment of joint disorder, most particularly in the spine, and the effects on the nervous system. The main difference between a chiropractor and an osteopath is that the former is more likely to use standard orthodox orthopaedic and neurological tests and X-rays.

Colour therapy

Interest in colour therapy is growing. Interior designers are often called in by large organisations in order to design an interior with a colour scheme that is conducive to work (in the work area) and rest (in the staff room).

Some hospitals are now taking account of the fact that regulation hospital green did nothing to help people get well and are building bright, cheerful colours into some areas and restful, peaceful colours into others.

While it has long been known that there are psychological reactions to colour (browns and greys can be drab and depressing), the effect of artificial light as opposed to natural light is also an issue. Many people who work in environments dependent upon artificial light complain that this affects their health.

Dance therapy

Dance therapy has been used in hospitals for people with mental health problems since the Second World War. It works in a variety of ways, such as facilitating the expression of emotions, releasing tension, providing some physical contact, developing and releasing energy, and finding a sense of personal rhythm. It is believed that dance therapy gives a sense of bodily awareness to those who are extremely withdrawn, such as autistic children.

Attending dance classes, particularly those with therapy as an objective, can provide many benefits to people who experience mental health problems, not least helping them overcome loneliness.

Drama therapy

Drama therapy incorporates techniques such as role-play, observation and experimenting with different ways of dealing with a situation in order to help people deal with emotional difficulties. It can help build self-confidence and social abilities as well as enable people to have fun while learning something about themselves, their feelings and their relationships.

Dream work

Dream therapy helps people to understand their dreams, not by imposing a therapist's interpretation of the dream, but in a way that makes sense of the imagery and symbols to the dreamer. A record is kept of the dream or dreams, and these are fed back to others in the group, who will also share their dreams.

Exercise

Exercise releases 'nature's natural painkillers', endorphins, it uses up adrenaline and other hormones which are produced under stress, and so helps us to relax, as well as strengthening our heart and improving circulation. Research suggests that vigorous exercise can lead to biochemical changes within our bodies that improve our psychological as well as physical well-being. Exercise can help us sleep better, develop our strength and self-esteem, and reduce anxiety and depression.

If you are very unfit, over 35 or have been unwell, it is important to take the advice of your GP before choosing to embark on strenuous exercise, however. As well as checking you out, some more radical GPs will actually prescribe suitable exercise at the local health centre for you.

If you feel up to improving your level of exercise and fitness, seek out some form of input to give you help, guidance and support. If the cost of some forms of exercise is too expensive, try to walk, swim or dance for 20–30 minutes, three times a week

Feldenkrais technique

Another awareness through movement technique.

Flotation therapy

Sometimes known as restricted environment stimuli therapy, flotation therapy was developed by Dr John C. Lilley, a trainee psychoanalyst, in 1954. He found that very deep levels of relaxation could be achieved by minimising the impact of the environment on the nervous system. Flotation therapy involves entering a flotation tank which is filled with about a foot of water treated with Epsom salts. This enables you to float on the water's surface, which is maintained at body temperature. You float for 50 minutes in darkness and silence, or to the sound of a relaxation tape. The experience has been shown to aid relaxation. Heart and breathing slow down, the electrical activity of the brain lessens and muscular pain is reduced.

Herbalism

Many, many years ago, people relied upon their instinct in order to understand which plants and herbs were safe to eat and which had healing properties. Much of this instinct has now been lost to us, drowned out by the din of expertise. However, the knowledge and use of herbs for medicinal purposes have been passed down through generations, and it was from these natural remedies that many of today's synthetic drugs were developed.

Herbalism, like many alternative treatments, has found it difficult to compete with the credibility of modern drugs. Commerce and marketing have vastly influenced the use and overuse of drugs. Multi-million pound businesses rely upon doctors taking up their products and prescribing them to patients, sometimes with disastrous results, as the side-effects of psychotropic drugs described in Chapter 7 show.

However, there is now a new interest in herbal and natural remedies. For example, according to Geoff Watts in an article for *World Medicine,* evening primrose oil is believed to have a positive effect on many complaints, including schizophrenia and alcoholism.

Ginseng, although still controversial, has for years been prescribed in China for depression as well as a range of other complaints. One of the difficulties in validating clinical trials has been the fact that a herbal remedy's efficaciousness relies not only on the individual but on their mood at the time. However, as many doctors and nurses working in the mental health field will know, the effectiveness of potent drugs such as Haloperidol, Chlorpromazine and Lorazepam also depend on the individual and their mood at the time. And while people who become very depressed may well need a course of anti-depressants as part of a care regime to get them well, herbal remedies such as evening primrose oil and ginseng may play a useful part in keeping them well.

Other herbs associated with the alleviation of mental health problems are:

Alcoholism – Cannabis(!), cayenne, feverfew, fringe tree, gold-enseal, mother of thyme, nerve root, passion flower, quassia, redcurrant and yellow jasmine
Depression – Sage (sometimes clary sage)
Insomnia – Anise, balm, dandelion, dill, hawthorn, mother of thyme, primrose, rosemary and many more
Nervous conditions (including restlessness, agitation and anxiety) – Almond, balm, borage, celery, hawthorn, jasmine, nerve root, pansy, passion flower, rosemary, sage, thyme, witch hazel and many more

Many physical conditions that might well have implications for our mental well-being can be helped with herbs. For a better understanding of herbalism, *The Herb Book* by John Lust (Bantam Books) provides a thoroughly comprehensive guide.

Hydrotherapy

The value of water as a therapeutic medium has been recognised for thousands of years. Whether used in massage, in the form of steam in Turkish baths, combined with massage in thalassotherapy, taken internally or bathed in (spa waters, swimming, jacuzzis or just lying in the bath), water can make us feel good and in some cases may have other properties (minerals, heat) that make it more effective.

Ionisation therapy

Some air molecules (a few thousand out of millions) carry either positive or negative electrical charges. These are known as *ions*. In order for an atmosphere to be healthy, ions should be in balance or negatively charged. When there is a preponderance of positive ions, people can feel the effects, often in the form of headaches and depression. Stormy weather, some winds, polluted air and central heating systems can all act to disturb the ion balance.

Air ionisers are available in health stores and by mail order and work by restoring the balance of positive and negative ions in the air. Research has yet to turn up any negative effects of ionisers.

Massage

Touch is very important to our mental well-being and a range of therapies use it, Rolfing, physiotherapy and shiatsu being just a few. Massage itself is not usually seen as a therapy, although its effects can certainly be very therapeutic.

It works with the soft tissues of the body, inducing relaxation through their handling. Massage is also therapeutic because of the pleasurable warm feelings it can produce.

Ideally, masseurs should be skilled at building rapport with their clients. As a full body massage can take an hour, conversation with the masseur should also contribute to a feeling of well-being.

Massage is more widely available than many other types of touch therapies and many masseurs are able to come to your home.

Music therapy

Most of us at some time have put on a record or tape of music we know will make us cheer up or feel sad, and so music as a therapy may seem to be stretching a therapeutic point. However, as a non-verbal method of communication and expression music has much to offer people with emotional difficulties and other forms of mental health problems.

Reflexology

Reflexologists work with the patient's feet, identifying build-ups of crystalline deposits and massaging areas of the feet to break these up and allow them to be disposed of through the body's own waste disposal system. This allows blocked energy flows to work more freely.

Different parts of the feet relate to the energy flow to different parts of the body. The massage is often very gentle, although if deeper pressure is needed due to the nature or extent of the block some very brief but quite severe pain can be experienced.

Reflexology can be very relaxing and stress-reducing. It can also deal with a wide range of physical complaints, including constipation, diabetes, headaches, glandular disease and hypertension, all of which can have spin-off effects for our mental health.

The French philosopher Rousseau once said that the doctor's job was to keep the patient entertained until nature took its course and healing took place. In the same vein reflexologists believe that the body heals itself and that the therapist just acts as a mediator between you and your body's natural healing powers.

Rolfing

Rolfing is a physical therapy that frees the mind and emotions as well as the body from past conditioning. It has as its base massage or manipulation. The emphasis of the manipulation is on the body's connective tissue and muscle. It is in this way that Rolfing differs from other manipulative therapies that concentrate on the spine.

Again, physical alignment is important. If alignment is out because of physical or emotional trauma or just bad posture, the muscles and connective tissues suffer. This in turn has a negative effect on the body and mind as a whole.

Dr Ida Rolf, the creator of Rolfing, believed that our emotions cause postural change and this can be witnessed in people who are unhappy or depressed – their head is down, shoulders are rounded, chest closed in – or angry – the body is tense, rigid. By rebalancing the physical self, the emotional self is enhanced through catharsis (the release of emotional pain) and behaviour and attitudes can be changed.

Rolfers work by photographing both the front and back of the client's body before the course begins and then at the end of each session.

During the session, the Rolfer uses fingertips, knuckles and sometimes elbows to free shortened connective tissue. The whole body is worked on, often with an early emphasis on the legs and feet to improve the client's balance and allow them to feel more 'centred'. The majority of sessions (a course usually consists of 10 individual sessions) concentrate on individual sections of the body while the last few are designed to realign and reintegrate the whole body.

Shiatsu

Shiatsu is the Japanese word for 'finger pressure'. It can been seen as acupuncture without needles, as it uses points along meridians or energy flows within the body. Unlike acupuncture, which is rarely self-administered, shiatsu can also be a form of self-help, as it is possible to apply finger pressure to accessible parts of the body.

It is often quite natural for us to do this in any case. We rub our eyes when they are tired and parts of our head and neck when we have a headache or are very tense. In fact shiatsu is very good for stress disorders.

Courses in shiatsu are becoming increasingly common and may well be offered at a local adult education centre or be advertised in the local paper.

T'ai chi

T'ai chi is a kind of meditation on the move. Using ritual movements and exercises, its emphasis is on psychological and spiritual development.

To watch, it looks similar to a martial art in its movements, although they are slow, smooth and fluid. Both trance-like and dance-like, they create a very deep relaxation to a point where a floating sensation can be induced. It is not difficult to imagine how restful and health promoting such a feeling must be.

Again, like shiatsu, T'ai chi is becoming increasingly popular in the Western world.

Yoga

Although some forms of yoga are deeply spiritual and take a religious dedication to master, there are other forms that are not so demanding. The main aim of yoga is to create a healthy mind in a healthy body. It has been proven scientifically that by using a combination of postures and controlled breathing, yoga reduces tension.

Yoga is best learnt with a qualified teacher although it is possible to obtain books explaining postures and breathing techniques from libraries and bookshops. Many adult education centres offer classes at reasonable prices with discounts for people who are unemployed.

RESOURCES

Publications

Care in the community

Baldock, John, and Ungerson, Clare, *Becoming Consumers of Community Care*, Joseph Rowntree, 1994

Bean, Philip, and Mounser, Patricia, *Discharged from Mental Hospitals*, Mind/Macmillan, 1992

Bornat, Pereira, Pilgrim & Williams, eds, *Community Care: A reader*, Macmillan/OUP, 1993

Grimshaw, Catherine, *A to Z of your Rights under the NHS and Community Care Legislation*, Mind, 1993

Hughes, Beverley, *Older People and Community Care*, Open University Press, 1995

Morgan, Steve, *Community Mental Health*, Chapman & Hall, 1994

Ramon, Shulamit, ed., *Beyond Community Care*, Mind/Macmillan, 1991

Vaughan, Phillip J., and Badger, Douglas, *Working with the Mentally Disordered Offender in the Community*, Chapman & Hall, 1995

Villeneau, Louise, *Housing with Care and Support*, Mind, 1992

Wertheimer, Alison, *Housing: The foundation of community care*, Mind/NFHA, 1989

Child abuse

Ainscough, Carolyn, and Toon, Kay, *Breaking Free: Help for survivors of child sexual abuse*, Sheldon Press, 1993

Miller, Alice, *Breaking Down the Wall of Silence*, Virago, 1993

Smith, Gerrilyn, *The Protectors' Handbook*, The Women's Press, 1995

Walker, Moira, *Surviving Secrets*, Open University Press, 1992

Drugs and treatments

Breggin, Peter, *Toxic Psychiatry: A psychiatrist speaks out*, HarperCollins, 1993

Cohen, David, ed., *Challenging the Therapeutic State, Part Two: Further disquisitions on the mental health system*, JMB, 1995

Cooper, Judy, and Lewis, Jenny, *Who Can I Talk To? The user's guide to therapy and counselling*, Headway, 1995

Copeland, Mary Ellen, *Living without Depression and Manic Depression*, New Harbinger Publications, 1995

Dinnage, Rosemary, *One to One: Experiences of psychotherapy*, Penguin, 1992

Drew, Tony, and King, Madeleine, *The Mental Health Handbook (DK): The complete guide to treatment, care and resources*, Piatkus, 1995

Dumont, Dr Matthew, *Therapists in the Community*, Jason Aronson Inc., 1995

Ernst, Sheila, and Goodison, Lucy, *In Our Own Hands: A book of self-help therapy*, The Women's Press, 1981

Holmes, Jeremy, *Between Art and Science*, Routledge, 1994

Jehu, D., *Patients as Victims: Sexual abuse in psychotherapy and counselling*, Wiley, 1994

Knight, Lindsay, *Talking to a Stranger: A consumer's guide to therapy*, Hodder & Stoughton, 1995

Kovel, Joe, *A Complete Guide to Therapy*, Penguin, 1992

Lacey, Ron, *The Complete Guide to Psychiatric Drugs: A layman's handbook*, Ebury Press/Mind, 1991

Lake, Tony, and Acheson, Fran, *Room to Listen, Room to Talk*, Bedford Square Press, 1988

Medawar, Charles, *Power and Dependence*, Social Audit, 1992

Morgan, Dr Robert F., *Electro Shock: The case against*, IPI, 1991

Murray, Russell, Hurle, Donna, and Grant, Anthony, *Tranquillizers: The Mind guide to where to get help*, Mind/Bradford University, 1991

Quilliam, S., and Grove-Stephenson, I., *The Counselling Handbook*, Thorsons, 1990

Wilde McCormick, Elizabeth, *Change for the Better: Self-help through practical psychotherapy*, Cassell, 1996

Woods, D., *The Power of Words: Uses and Abuses of Talking Treatments*, Mind, 1993

Eating distress

Buckroyd, Julia, *Anorexia and Bulimia*, Element Books, 1996

Cooper, Peter, *Bulimia Nervosa: A guide to recovery*, Robinson, 1993

Lawrence, Marilyn, *The Anorexic Experience*, The Women's Press, 1995

Lawrence, Marilyn, ed., *Fed Up and Hungry: Women, oppression and food*, The Women's Press, 1987

Orbach, Susie, *Hunger Strike*, Penguin, 1993

General

Barker, Philip J., and Baldwin, Steve, eds, *Ethical Issues in Mental Health*, Chapman & Hall, 1991

Butler, Gillian, and Hope, Tony, *Manage your Mind: The mental health fitness guide*, Oxford University Press, 1995

Chamberlin, Judi, *On Our Own*, Mind, 1988

Crichton, John, ed., *Psychiatric Patient Violence: Risk and response*, Duckworth, 1995

Directory of Mental Health Services for Refugees, The Refugee Council, 1995

Firth-Cozens, Jenny, *Audit in Mental Health Services*, LEA, 1994

Harding, Len, *Born a Number*, Mind, 1986

Hart, Linda, *Phone at Nine Just to Say You're Alive*, Douglas Elliot Press, 1995

Hunt, Marsha, *Repossessing Ernestine*, HarperCollins, 1996

Lyttle, Jack, *Mental Disorder*, Baillière Tindall, 1986

McIver, Shirley, *Obtaining the Views of Users of Health Services*, King's Fund, 1992

Newton, Jennifer, *Preventing Mental Illness in Practice*, Routledge, 1995

O'Hagan, Mary, *Stopovers on my Way Home from Mars*, Survivors Speak Out, 1993

Pilgrim, David, and Rogers, Anne, *A Sociology of Mental Health and Illness*, Open University Press, 1993

Read, Jim, and Wallcraft, Jan, *Guidelines on Advocacy for Mental Health Workers*, UNISON/Mind, 1995

Read, Jim, and Wallcraft, Jan, *Guidelines on Equal Opportunities and Mental Health*, UNISON/Mind, 1995

Rogers, Anne, Pilgrim, David, and Lacey, Ron, *Experiencing Psychiatry: Users' views of services*, Mind/Macmillan, 1993

Romme, Prof. Marius, and Escher, Sandra, *Accepting Voices*, Mind, 1993

Slater, Robert, *The Psychology of Growing Old*, Open University Press, 1995

Tilbury, Derek, *Working with Mental Illness*, Macmillan, 1993

Tudor, Keith, *Mental Health Promotion*, Routledge, 1996

Under the Asylum Tree: Survivors' Poetry, Survivors Speak Out, 1995

Warner, Richard, *Recovery from Schizophrenia*, Routledge, 1994

Mental health law

Alty, Ann, and Mason, Tom, *Seclusion and Mental Health*, Chapman & Hall, 1994

Jones, Richard, *Mental Health Act Manual*, Sweet & Maxwell, 1996

Gordon, Richard, *Community Care Assessments: A practical legal framework*, Longman, 1993

Gostin, Larry, and Fennell, Phil, *Mental Health: Tribune procedure*, Longman, 1992

Hoggett, Brenda, *Mental Health Law*, Sweet & Maxwell, 1990

Mental Health Handbook (Law): A guide to the law affecting children and young people, Children's Legal Centre, 1994

Prins, Herschel, *Offenders, Deviants or Patients?*, Routledge, 1995

Staite, Catherine, *et al.*, *Diversion from Custody for Mentally Disordered Offenders*, Pennant, 1996

Whitehorn, Norman, *Court of Protection Handbook*, Oyez Longman, 1988

Race and mental health

Fernando, Suman, ed., *Mental Health in a Multi-Ethnic Society*, Macmillan/Mind, 1995

Lago, Colin, *Race, Culture and Counselling*, Open University Press, 1996

Littlewood, Roland, and Lipsedge, Maurice, *Aliens and Alienists*, Routledge, 1989

Rack, Philip, *Race, Culture and Mental Disorder*, Tavistock, 1982

Webb Johnson, Amanda, *A Cry for Change*, CIO, 1991

Wilson, Melba, *Mental Health and Britain's Black Communities*, King's Fund, 1993

Support and care

Burningham, Sally, *Not on your Own: The Mind Guide to Mental Health*, Penguin, 1989

Chadwick, Dr Peter, *Understanding Paranoia*, Thorsons, 1995

Cleghorn, Patricia, *The Secrets of Self-Esteem*, Element Books, 1996

Forward, Dr Susan, *Toxic Parents: Overcoming their hurtful legacy and reclaiming your life*, Bantam Books, 1990

Gray Davidson, Frena, *Alzheimer's: A practical guide to help you through the day*, Piatkus, 1995

Horwood, Janet, *Caring: How to cope*, HEA, 1994

Madders, Jane, *Stress and Relaxation*, Macdonald Optima, 1981

Markham, Ursula, *Bereavement*, Element Books, 1996

Mortimer, Mary, *When your Partner Dies*, The Women's Press, 1995

Payne, Rosemary A., *Relaxation Techniques*, Churchill Livingstone, 1995

Rosenthal, Norman E., *Winter Blues*, Guildford Press, 1994

Rowe, Dorothy, *Depression: The way out of your prison*, Routledge, 1983

Sheehan, Elaine, *Anxiety, Phobias and Panic Attacks*, Element Books, 1996

Smith, Gerrilyn, and Nairne, Kathy, *Dealing with Depression*, The Women's Press, 1995

Toates, Frederick, *Obsessive Compulsive Disorder: What it is and how to deal with it*, Thorsons, 1990

Ward, Barbara, *Healing Grief: A guide to loss and recovery*, Vermilion, 1993

Wertheimer, Alison, *A Special Scar*, Routledge, 1991

Wilde McCormick, Elizabeth, *Breakdown*, Optima, 1993

Women, men and gender

Abel, Kathryn, *et al.*, *Planning Community Mental Health Services for Women*, Routledge, 1996

Barnes, Marian, and Maple, Norma, *Women and Mental Health: Challenging the stereotypes*, Venture Press, 1992

Busfield, Joan, *Men, Women and Madness: Understanding Gender and Mental Disorder*, Macmillan, 1996

Davies, Dominic, and Neal, Charles, eds, *Pink Therapy*, Oxford

University Press, 1996

Mason-John, Valerie, ed., *Talking Black*, Cassell, 1995

Meth, R. L., and Pasick, R., *Men in Therapy: The challenge of change*, Guildford Press, 1994

O'Connor, Noreen, and Ryan, Joanna, *Wild Desires and Mistaken Identities*, Virago, 1993

Rutter, Peter, *Sex in the Forbidden Zone*, Mandala, 1991

Ussher, Jane, *Women's Madness: Misogyny or mental illness*, Harvester Wheatsheaf, 1991

Zaki, Mary, Craig, Judith, *et al.*, *Inside Outside*, Outsider Publications, 1995

Young people

Burningham, Sally, *Young People under Stress*, Mind/Virago, 1994

David, Tricia, ed., *Working Together for Young Children*, Routledge, 1994

Hill, Kate, *The Long Sleep: Young people and suicide*, Virago, 1995

Rioch, Sheila, *Suicidal Children and Adolescents*, Celia Publications, 1994

Spandler, Helen, *Who's Hurting Who? Young people, self-harm and suicide*, 42nd Street, 1996

Magazines

OpenMind, Mind magazine, published every two months; details available from Mind.

Advice booklets

Mind publishes advice booklets giving straightforward practical information on a range of mental health issues, from understanding therapy to mental health law. Reports and information packs on particular topics are also available, including:

A–Z of Complementary and Alternative Therapies, Mind, 1995

A–Z of Race Issues in Mental Health, Mind, 1996

Baker, Paul, *The Voice Inside*, Hearing Voices Network, 1995

Code of Practice: Mental Health Act 1983, HMSO, 1993

Counselling and Psychotherapy: Is it for me? The British Association of Counselling

Croft, Suzy, and Beresford, Peter, *Getting Involved: A practical manual*, Open Services Project, 1993

Gorman, Janet, *Out of the Shadows*, Mind, 1992

Knowing Our Own Minds: A survey of how people in emotional distress take control of their lives, The Mental Health Foundation, 1997

Leader, Alan, *Direct Power*, CSN/BCS/Mind/Pavilion, 1995

Lindow, Vivien, *Self-Help Alternatives to Mental Health Services*, Mind, 1994

Lodge, Dr Brian, *Coping with Caring*, Mind, 1981

Mental Health Act 1983: An outline guide, Mind

The Mind Guide to Advocacy in Mental Health Empowerment in Action, Mind, 1992

The Mind Guide to Managing Stress, Mind, 1995

Mind Practice Guidelines Pack, Mind, 1994

Mind Quality Guidelines Pack, Mind, 1994

Mind's Policy on Black and Minority Ethnic People and Mental Health, Mind, 1993

Mind's Policy on Physical Treatments, Mind, 1994

Mind's Policy on Talking Treatments, Mind, 1994

Not Just Black and White, GPMH, 1995

Pembroke, Louise Roxanne, ed., *Self-Harm: Perspectives from personal experience*, Survivors Speak Out, 1994

The Power of Words, Mind, 1993

Purchasing Effective Mental Health Services for Women, University of Kent, 1993

Reshaping the Future: Mind's model for community mental health care, Mind, 1995

Safe and Effective? Mind, 1993

User Involvement Information Pack, South East Mind, 1990

Women and Mental Health: Mind policy paper, Mind, 1992

Women and Mental Health Information Pack, GPMH, 1994

USEFUL ADDRESSES

ACCEPT Services
724 Fulham Road
London SW6 5SE
0171–371 7477/7555

Age Concern (Northern Ireland)
3 Lower Crescent
Belfast
BT7 1NR
Tel: 01232 245729

Age Concern Cymru
1 Cathedral Road
Cardiff
CF1 9SD
Tel: 01222 371566

Age Concern England
Astral House
1268 London Road
London SW16 4ER
Tel: 0181–679 8000

Alcoholics Anonymous
PO Box 1
11 Stonebow House,
Stonebow, York
YO1 2NJ
Tel: 01904 644026

The Alzheimer's Disease Society (England)
Gordon House
10 Greencoat Place
Fulham Broadway
London SW1 1PH
Tel: 0171–306 0606

The Alzheimer's Disease Society (Family Counselling Service)
108 Battersea High Street
London SW11 3HP
Tel: 0171–223 7000

The Arbours Association
6 Church Lane
London N8 7BU
Tel: 0181–348 6466
(10a.m.–1p.m., Mon.–Fri.)

The Asian Family Counselling Service
74 The Avenue
West Ealing
London W13 8LB
Tel: 0181–997 5749

The British Acupuncture Association
34 Alderney Street
London SW18 4EU
Tel: 0171–134 1012/3353

The British Association for Counselling
1 Regent Place
Rugby
Warwickshire
CV21 2PJ
Tel: 01788 578328

The British Association of Psychotherapists
37 Mapsbury Road
London NW2 4HJ
Tel: 0181 452 9823

The British Confederation of Care Home Proprietors
840 Melton Road
Thurmaston
Leicester LE4 8BN
Tel: 0116–264 0095

The British Hypnotherapy Association
1 Wythburn Place
London W1H 5WL
Tel: 0181–723 4443

The British Psychological Society
St Andrew's House
48 Princes Road East
Leicester
LE1 7DR
Tel: 0116 549568

The Centre for Stress Management
156 Westcombe Hill
London SE3 7DH
Tel: 0181–293 4114

Depression Alliance
PO Box 1022
London SE1 7GR
Tel: 0181–721 7672

Drinkline
Weddel House
13–14 West Smithfield
London EC1A 9DL
Tel: 0171–332 0150

Drugline
28 Ballina Street
London SE23 1DR
Tel: 0171–291 2341

The Eating Disorders Association
Sackville Place
44 Magdalen Street
Norwich
NR3 1JU
Tel: 01603 621414

The Ex-Services Mental Welfare Society
Broadway House
The Broadway
London SW19 1RL
Tel: 0181–543 6333

The Fellowship of Depressives Anonymous
36 Chestnut Avenue
Beverley
North Humberside
HU17 9QU
Tel: 01482 860619

Gamblers Anonymous
PO Box
London SW10 0EU
Tel: 0171–352 3060

The General Council and Register of Consultant Herbalists
Marlborough House
Swanpool
Falmouth
Cornwall
TR11 4HW
Tel: 01326 317321

Gestalt Centre London
64 Warwick Road
St Albans
Herts
AL1 4DL
Tel: 01727 864 806

**Greater London Alcohol
Advisory Service**
30–31 Great Sutton Street
London EC1V 0DX
Tel: 0171–250 1627

Guideposts Trust
Two Rivers, Station Lane
Whitney
Oxon OX8 6BH
Tel: 01993 772886

**Guildford Centre and
Society for Psychotherapy**
PO Box 63
Guildford
Surrey
GU1 2U2
Tel: 01483 560 607

Hearing Voices Network
c/o Creative Support
16 Tariff Street
Manchester M1 2EP
Tel: 0161–228 3896

**The Hypnotherapy
Association of Qualified
Curative Hypnotherapists**
10 Balaclava Road
Kings Heath
Birmingham
Tel: 0121–444 5435

**The Institute for
Complementary Medicine**
21 Portland Place
London W1N 3AF
Tel: 0171–636 9543

**The Institute of Family
Therapy**
24–32 Stephenson Way
London NW1 4HX
Tel: 0171–391 9150

**The Institute of Group
Analysis**
1 Daleham Gardens
London NW3 5BY
Tel: 0171–435 6455

**The International Register
of Oriental Medicine**
Green Hedges House
Green Hedges Avenue
East Grinstead
East Sussex
RH19 1DZ
Tel: 01342 313106/7

**The International Stress
Management Association**
South Bank University
103 Borough Road
London SE1 0AA
Tel: 0171–258 4025

The Law Society
113 Chancery Lane
London WC2A 1PL
Tel: 0171–242 1222

The Life Care NHS Trust
Coulsdon Road
Caterham
Surrey CR3 5YA
Tel: 01883 346411

**The Manic Depression
Fellowship**
81 High Street
Kingston upon Thames
KT1 1EY
Tel: 0181–974 6550

**The Mental After Care
Association**
25 Bedford Square
London WC1B 3HW
Tel: 0171–436 6194

**The Mental Health Act
Commission**
Maid Marian House
56 Hounds Gate
Nottingham
NG1 6BG
Tel: 01602 504040

**The Mental Health
Foundation**
37 Mortimer Street
London W1N 8JU

Mind
Granta House
15–19 Broadway
Stratford
London E15 4BQ
Tel: 0181–519 2122

NAFSIYAT
Inter-Cultural Therapy
Centre
278 Seven Sisters Road
Finsbury Park
London N4 2HY
Tel: 0171–263 4130

**The National Association
for Patient Participation**
Hazelbank
Peaselake
Guildford
Surrey
GU5 9RJ

**The National Council of
Psychotherapists and
Hypnotherapy Register**
1 Clovelly Road
Ealing
London W5
Tel: 0181–840 3790

The National Institute of Medical Herbalists
41 Hatherley Road
Winchester
Hampshire
SO22 6RR

The National Institute of Reflexology
29 Hollyfield Avenue
London N11 3BY
Tel: 0171–368 0865

The National Schizophrenia Fellowship (England)
28 Castle Street
Kingston upon Thames
KT1 1SS
Tel: 0181–547 3937

The National Schizophrenia Fellowship (Northern Ireland)
Wyndhurst
Knockbracken Healthcare Park
Smithfield Road
Belfast
BT8 8BH

The Northern Schizophrenia Fellowship
38 Collingwood Buildings
Collingwood Street
Newcastle upon Tyne
Tyne and Wear
NE1 1JH
Tel: 01632 614343

Nottingham Advocacy Group
65 Birkin Avenue
Hyson Green
Nottingham

PACE
34 Hartham Road
London N7 9JL

The Philadelphia Association
4 Marty's Yard
17 Hampstead High Street
London NW3 1QW
Tel: 0171–794 2652

Phobics Action
Hornbeam House
Claybury Grounds
Manor Road
Woodford Green
Essex
Tel: 0181–559 2551

Prevention of Professional Abuse Network (POPAN)
Flat 1
20 Daleham Gardens
London NW3 5DA

Psychiatric Rehab Association
Bayford Mews
Bayford Street
London E8 3SF
Tel: 0181–985 3570

The Reflexology Association
Slaters
14 Willows End
London SE3 9JL
Tel: 0181–852 6062

The Register of Traditional Chinese Medicine
7a Thorndean Street
London SW18 4HE

The Research Council for Complementary Medicine
Suite 1
19a Cavendish Square
London W1
Tel: 0171–493 6930

The Richmond Fellowship
8 Addison Road
London W14 8DL
Tel: 0171–603 6373

The SAD (Seasonal Affective Disorder) Association
PO Box 989
London SW7 2PZ
Tel: 01903 814942

St Mungo's
Atlantic House
1–3 Rockley Road
London W14 ODJ
Tel: 0181–740 9968

Survivors Speak Out
33 Lichfield Road
London NW2

The Traditional Acupuncture Society
11 Grange Park
Stratford upon Avon
Warwickshire
CV37 6XH

Triumph over Phobia (Top UK)
PO Box 1831
Bath
BA1 3TX
Tel: 01225 330 353

The United Kingdom Council for Psychotherapy
Regent's College
Inner Circle
Regent's Park
London NW1 4NS
Tel: 0171–487 7554

The Westminster Pastoral Foundation
23 Kensington Square
London W8 5HN
Tel: 0171–937 6956

INDEX

abreaction 70
abuse (by therapists) 82–3
ACCEPT 11
accommodation 88–91
acrophobia 9
acupressure 133
acupuncture 15, 132–3
additives, food (E) 59, 60
Adler, Alfred 71
advocacy 104, 120
   citizen 120
   paid 120
   patient 120
   self- 120–2
aerophobia 9
afraid, fear of being 9
Age Concern 89
aggression 30, 32, 43, 68–9
   redirecting 32–3
   sociopathic 34
agitation 14, 43, see also anxiety
agoraphobia 1, 7–8
Aikido 53, 133
ailurophobia 9
air ionisers 142
Akineton 126
akithisia 126
Al-Anon Family Groups 11
Alateen 11
alcohol/alcoholism 1, 3–4, 10–12, 31,
   35, 42, 43, 56–9, 80
   and alternative treatments 133, 134,
    142
   and aversion therapy 75
   and depression 20, 59
   and relaxation 48, 64
Alcohol Concern 11, 12
Alcoholics Anonymous 11, 80
Alexander technique 133
algophobia 9
Allegron 127
allergies 60, 134
Almazine 128
alone, fear of being 9
Alprazolam 128
alternative treatments 132–46
altruism 55

Alupram 129
Alzheimer's disease 17, 18
Amitriptyline 127
Anafranil 127
anger 32, 43
   working off 32–3, 54, 134
animals, fear of 9
Anorexia Anonymous 13
anorexia nervosa 12–13, 76, 134
Anorexic Aid 13
Anorexic Family Aid 13
anthroposophical medicine 133–4
anti-depressants 15, 16, 21
   MAOI 128
   reactions to 23
   tricyclic 127–8
anxiety 5, 13–15, 18, 25, 30, 31
   controlling 49, 50
Anxon 129
apiphobia 9
appetite, lack of 21, 61
applied kinesiology 134
arachnophobia 10
Arbours Association 84, 90
aromatherapy 134
art therapy 96, 98, 134
assertiveness training 74, 135
astrapophobia 9
Atensine 129
Ativan 128
auditory hallucinations 4, 5, 36
autogenic training 135
autophobia 9
Aventyl 127
aversion therapy 74–5

BAC see British Association for
   Counselling
Bach flower remedies 135–8
bacteria, fear of (bacteriaphobia) 9
batrachophobia 9
bed-sitting rooms 89
beer 58–9
bees, fear of 9
behaviour changes 17, 18
behaviour therapies 8, 30, 73–6
belenophobia 10

Benzotropine 126
bereavement 1, 15–17, 93
Berkomine 127
biofeedback 138
biofunctional therapy 73
Biperiden 126
birds, fear of 9
blindness, hysterical 5
blood, fear of 9
blues: baby 27
'winter' *see* seasonal affective disorder
blushing, fear of 9
Bolvidon 127
breathing: laboured 126
    and relaxation 48–9, *see also* yoga
Bristol Crisis Service for Women 33
British Association for Counselling
    (BAC) 83
    Counselling and Psychotherapy
    Resources Directory 81
British Confederation of Care Home
    Proprietors 89, 91
Bromazepam 128
bulimia nervosa 13, 17
buried alive, fear of being 9
Butryptyline 127

caffeine 59
Canadian Mental Health Association:
    ways to deal with tension 54–5
cancer, fear of (cancerophobia) 9
cardiophobia 9
care homes 89, 91
care plans 87, 98, 100
care programme approach 87–8, 100,
    116
    and patient involvement 98
carers 80, 93
    respite care for 90
cats, fear of 9
Centrax 129
checking rituals, compulsive 24–5
childbirth: fear of 9
    see also post-natal depression
chiropractic 138
Chlordiazepoxide 129
Chlorpromazine 23, 125, 141
Chlorprothixene 125
chocolate 59
cider 58
cirrhosis 11
Citizen's Advice Bureaux 65, 87, 90, 91
classifications, mental health 4–7
claustrophobia 7

cleaning, compulsive 25
clinical psychologists 33, 97–8
Clobazepam 129
Clomipramine 127
Clopenthixol 125, 126
Clopixol 125, 126
Clorazepate 129
'cluster' flats 90
coffee 59
Cogentin 126
cognitive behaviour therapies 76
cognitive therapy 30
coitophobia 10
Coker, Ade 35
'collective unconscious' 71
colleges: counselling services 84
colour therapy 138–9
community care 85, 99
    and housing schemes 95–6
    necessary conditions for 85–6
community meetings 120
community mental health (psychiatric)
    nurses 33, 87, 96, 97
Compassionate Friends 16, 93
competitiveness 55
complaints, making 105, 122
    against therapists 82–3
compulsive behaviour 5, 24–5
concentration, poor 30, 43
Concordin 127
confidence *see* self-confidence
confidentiality, rights to 82, 105
confusion, toxic 17, 127, 129
constipation 24, 127, 144
consumerism/consumer movement
    119
contracts (in behaviour therapy) 75
corpses, fear of 9
counselling 8, 67, 68, 83, 84, 96
Creutzfeld's disease 17
criminals and offenders 99–100, 114–16
criticism 43, 55
crowds, fear of 9
CRUSE 16, 83
crying *see* tearfulness
cutting oneself 31, 32, 34
cynophobia 9

Dalmane 129
dance therapy 139
darkness, fear of 9
Dartalan 125
day classes 94
day hospitals 96

death: fear of 9
  see also bereavement
delusions, primary 36
dementia 17–19
  and alcohol 11
Depixol 125, 126
'depot' injections 96
depression 1, 5, 6, 19–22, 23–4, 79, 86
  and alcohol 20, 59
  alternative treatments for 141, 142
  and bereavement 15, 16
  and ECT treatment 130–1
  and sleeplessness 64–5
  see also manic depression; post-natal
    depression
desensitisation 75
Desipramine 127
despair, feelings of 21, 31
detoxification 11
diagnoses, mental health 4–5, 7
diarrhoea 14, 43, 129
Diazepam 126, 129
Dibenzepin 127
diet 20, 59–61, *see also* food
dirt, fear of 9
Disability Discrimination Act (1996) 92
discrimination 92
disease, fear of 9
Disipal 126
distonic reactions, acute 126
distorted perception 5–6
doctors *see* general practitioners
dogs, fear of 9
Dolmatil 125
Domical 127
Dopamine 37, 127
Dothiepin 127
Doxepin 127
drama therapy 139
dreams, fear of 9
dream work 139–40
drinks 59, *see also* alcohol
Droleptan 125
Droperidon 125
drowsiness 129
drug addiction 1, 134
drug treatment 66, 123–4
  anti-depressants 127–8
  major tranquillisers 23, 125–6
  minor tranquillisers 128–9
  paranoid reactions to 26
  and schizophrenic-type reactions 37
  side-effects of 124–9
dyskinesia, tardive 126

E additives 59, 60
eating: change in patterns 21, 61, 43
  distress *see* anorexia; bulimia
  see also diet
ECT *see* electro-convulsive therapy
Elavil 127
elderly people:
  accommodation for 89, 91
  and exercise 63
  and sleep 64
Elderly Accommodation Counsel Ltd
  89
electro-convulsive therapy (ECT) 22,
  25, 117, 118, 130–1
electroplexy 13, *see* electro-convulsive
  therapy
emotions (*see* anger *etc.*):
  and detachment 29
  inappropriate 36
employment 91–2
  and counselling 84
  voluntary 93–4
enclosed spaces, fear of 9
endorphins 140
energy, lack of 31
entomophobia 9
environmental effects 3, 7
erythrophobia 9
'escapism' 54
ethnic groups 35, 81
Euhypnos 129
euphoria, feelings of 22, 23
European Commission for Human
  Rights 103, 105–7
Evacalm 129
Evadyne 127
evening classes 94
evening primrose oil 141
exercise(s) 20, 50, 54, 61–4, 140
  relaxation 49–52
expression, disorder of 37

facial grimaces 126
faintness 128
family therapy 78–9
fantasy worlds, withdrawal into 37
fatigue 28, 42, 43, 133
Faverin 128
fear *see* agitation; anxiety; panic
  attacks; phobias
Feldenkrais technique 140
Fentazin 125
'fight or flight' response 14, 50
fire, fear of 9

flooding (therapy) 75
flotation therapy 140–1
flower remedies, Bach 135–8
Fluitrazepam 128
Flupenthixol 125
Flupenthixol decanoate 126
Fluphenazine decanoate 126
Fluphenazine enanthate 126
Flurazepam 129
Fluspirilene 126
Fluvoxamine 128
flying, fear of 9
food *see* diet; eating distress
  allergies 134
  and drugs 128
foreigners, fear of 9
free association 69
Freud, Sigmund 68–9, 71
friends, making 55, 92–4
Frisium 129
Fromm, Erich 71
fruit 60, 61

Gamanil 127
gambling 73
gamophobia 9
general practitioners 22, 96
  changing 104
genetic factors 7, 37
Gestalt therapy 71–2
Gingerbread 93
Ginseng 141
GPs *see* general practitioners
grieving *see* bereavement
group homes 89, 95
groups, support 92–3, 94
group therapy 76–7, 96, 98
guardianship orders 112–13
Guideposts 90
guilt, feelings of 21, 42, 44
gynophobia 10

haematophobia 9
haggard looks 43
Halcion 128
Haldol 125
Haldol decanoate 126
hallucinations 5
  alcohol-induced 11
  auditory 4, 5, 36
Haloperidol 23, 125, 141
Haloperidol decanoate 126
hands:
  shaky 43

sweaty 14, 43
washing constantly 25
wringing 14
headaches 138, 144
health care services *see* community
  care; National Health Service
heart disease, fear of 9
heights, fear of 9
helminthophobia 10
help, asking for 86–7
helplines 87, 94
Help the Aged 89
herbalism 15, 141–2
heredity 7, 37
Hidden Scars, Salisbury 33
hippophobia 9
hodophobia 10
homelessness *see* accommodation
homes, care 89, 91
homoeopathy 15
hopelessness 21, 31
horses, fear of 9
hospital orders 114
  interim 116
hospitals, day 96
hospitals, district general 95, 99
hospitals, psychiatric 94–5, 96, 99
  compulsory admission to 107–8,
    109–12
  decorating of 138–9
  discharge from 86, 87, 89, 105
  emergency admission to 111–12
  informal/voluntary admission to
    108, 109, 112
  mental health nurses 96–7
  multi-disciplinary teams 100
  patients' councils 119–20
  remand to 115–16
  secure 99–100
  therapies and therapists 95, 98
  ward rounds 100–2
hostels 89, 91, 95
hostility, feelings of 43
housing *see* accommodation
housing associations 89
human rights 103
  'assertive' 105–6
  European Commission for 103, 105
  and Patients' Charter 103, 104–5
  see also Mental Health Act (1983)
Huntington's chorea 17
hydrophobia 10
hydrotherapy 142
hyperactivity 60

hypertension 144
hyperventilation 49
hypnophobia 10
hypnosis 13
hypnotherapy 14, 73
hypothalamus 50
hysterical illnesses 5

illness, fear of 9
Imipramine 127
implosion (therapy) 75
industrial therapy 98
information, rights to 104
see also medical records
insanity, fear of 9
insects, fear of 9
insight 70
insomnia *see* sleeplessness
Integrin 125
interpreting services 104
involuntary movements 126
ionisation therapy 142
Iprindole 127
Iproniazid 128
irritability 30, 43
Isocarboxazid 128

Janov, Dr Arthur 72
jaw, stiff 43, 126
Jungian psychotherapy 71
katagelophobia 10
Kemadrin 126
keraunophobia 10
Ketazolam 129
'keyworkers' 87
kinesiology, applied 134

lager 58–9
Largactyl 125
Lentizol 127
LeShan, Lawrence: *How to Meditate* 53
Lexotan 128
Librium 129
Life Care and Housing Trust 90–1
light:
    artificial, and health 139
    fear of 9
    and seasonal affective disorder 31
lightning, fear of 9
Lilley, Dr John C. 140
lithium carbonate 23, 24, 129
lobotomies 117
local authorities 87
Lofepramine 127

loneliness 79, 139
Lorazepam 128, 141
Lormetazepam 128
Ludiomil 127
Lust, John: *The Herb Book* 142
lyssophobia 9
Lyttle, Jack: *Mental Disorder* 56
Madders, Jane: *Stress and Relaxation . . .* 53
'maladaptive' behaviour 5
mania 1, 22–3, 24, 118
manic depression 6, 23–4, 35
Manic Depression Fellowship 24
mantras 53
MAOI anti-depressants 128
Maprotiline 127
marital therapy 79
Marplan 128
marriage, fear of 9
Marriage Guidance Council *see* Relate
Marsilid 128
massage 52–3, 143, 144
Medazepam 129
medical records, access to 105, 119
medication *see* drug treatment
meditation 53
mellissophobia 9
memory loss 17, 18, 43
Mental After Care Association 90
Mental Health Act 1983 95, 103, 107–9, 122
    Section 2 109–10
    Section 3 87, 110–11
    Section 4 111–12, 117
    Sections 5.2 and 5.4 108, 112, 117
    Sections 7–10 112–13
    Section 25 113
    Section 35 115–16, 117
    Section 36 116
    Section 37 114
    Section 38 116
    Section 41 114–15
    Section 47 115
    Section 49 115
    Section 57 117
    Section 117 87
    Section 131 109
    Section 135 113–14, 117
    Section 136 113, 117
Mental Health Act Commission 122
mental health centres 96
mental health (psychiatric) nurses 96–7
Merital 127
Mianserin 127

microphobia 9
Mind 2, 25, 33, 85, 87, 90, 92, 93, 95, 97, 107, 124
mind control, fear of 5, 36
Modecate 126
modelling 75
Moditen 126
Mogadon 129
Molipaxin 127
monoamine oxidase inhibitors 128
monophobia 9
mood swings 20, 31
   and diet 59–60
motivation, lack of 28, 42
mouth:
   dry 14, 43, 127
   metallic taste in 129
   multi-disciplinary teams 100–2
   muscle movements, uncontrollable 126
   muscle relaxation 49–52
   music therapy 143
   mysophobia 9

nail biting 43
Nardil 128
National Confederation of Registered Residential Care Home Associations 89, 91
National Health Service 33, 83, 119
National Tranquilliser Advisory Council (Tranx) 22
nausea 43, 129
necrophobia 9
neglecting appearance 20, 43
neo-Freudian analysis 71
neologisms, use of 37
nervous conditions: herbal remedies 142
Neulactil 125
neuroleptic drugs 126
neuroses 5, 7
nightmares 29, 43
Nitrazepam 129
Nitrodos 129
Nobrium 129
Noctamid 128
Nomifensine 127
Normison 129
Nortriptyline 127
Norval 127
nosophobia 9
Noveril 127
nurses, mental health 33, 87, 96–7

nyctophobia 9

obsessive disorders 5, 24–5
occupational therapy 96, 98
ochlophobia 9
offenders, criminal 99–100, 114–16
oils, essential 134
oneirophobia 9
Open Door 83
Open Mind 52, 66
operant conditioning 76
operations, surgical 117
Orap 125
organic food 60–1
ornithophobia 9
Orphenadrine 126
osteopaths 138
osteoporosis 62
overdoses, taking 31
overeating 31
overstress 42
overwork 31, 55
Oxazepam 128
Oxypertine 125

pain, fear of 9
palpitations 43
panic attacks 8, 14, 43
paradoxical intention 76
paranoia 25–6
   and alcohol 11
   and dementia 18
Parazepam 129
Parkinson-like conditions 127
Parnate 128
passivity experience 36
pathophobia 9
Patients' Charter 103, 104–5
patients' councils 119–20
perfection, illusions of 39–40, 55
Pericyazine 125
Perls, Frederick (Fritz) 71
Perphenazine 125
persecution, feelings of 26, 36
personality changes 17, 18
personality disorder 5, 6
Pertofran 127
Phenelzine 128
Phenothiazines 126
phobias 1, 5, 7, 8–10
phobophobia 9
photophobia 9
Pick's disease 17
Pimozide 125

Piportil depot 126
Pipothiazine palmitate 126
plants, use of *see* Bach flower remedies;
    herbalism
police: and hospital admission 113–14
post-natal depression 1, 26–9
post-traumatic stress disorder 29–30
posture 21, 133, 144
'power to convey' 113
Praminil 127
preservatives, food 59, 60
primal therapy 72
prison, transfers from 115
privacy, rights to 105, 106
Prochloroperazine 125
Procyclidine 126
progesterone 28
Promazine 125
Prondol 127
Prothiaden 127
Protriptyline 127
psychiatric hospitals *see* hospitals,
    psychiatric
Psychiatric Rehabilitation Association
    90, 92
psychiatrists 97
psychoanalysis 68–70, 83
psychoanalytic psychotherapy 70
psychologists, clinical 97–8
psychopaths 6, *see* sociopaths
psychoses 5–6, 7
puerperal 27
psycho-sexual counselling 79
psychosomatic disorders 5
and aromatherapy 134
psychotherapy 8, 66–8, 83–4
    analytic 68–71
    post-analytic 71–3
puerperal psychosis 27
pyrophobia 9

quarrels: and stress 54

race: and schizophrenia 35–6
reality, loss of 5
rebelliousness, feelings of 43
Redeptin 126
reflexology 143–4
registers, supervision 116
rehabilitation services, hospital 95
Relate 79, 83
relationships, making 92–4
relationship therapy 79
relaxation 14

and breathing 48–9
deep muscle 50–2
exercises 49–50
and flotation therapy 140–1
and massage 52–3, 143
and meditation 53
and self-hypnosis 52
and yoga 53–4, 145–6
relaxation groups 93
reminiscence therapy 98
Remploy 92
repetitive actions and thoughts 24–5
reptiles, fear of 9
research trials, participation in 82,
    104–5
residential homes 89, 91
respite care 90
restricted environment stimuli therapy
    140–1
restriction orders 114–15
retrocollis 126
rewards and treats 20, 64
Richmond Fellowship 91, 92
ridicule, fear of 10
rights *see* human rights
rigidity, physical 127
rituals, compulsive 24–5
Roche 129
Rogerian therapy 72–3
Rohypnol 128
Rolfing 143, 144
Rosenhan, D. L. 36

SAD *see* seasonal affective disorder
St Mungo Hostel and Care Services 90,
    92
salt 59
Salvation Army 89, 91
Samaritans 16, 33, 94
Saroten 127
SASS *see* special assessment and
    supervision service unit
Satan, fear of (Satanophobia) 10
schizophrenia 1, 5, 6, 26, 35–8, 84
    and drugs 127
    and herbal therapy 141
schools: counselling services 84
scopophobia 9
seasonal affective disorder 30–1
'second opinions' 104, 107, 122
'Sectioning' *see* Mental Health Act
    (1983)
secure hospitals 99–100
self-advocacy 120–2

self-care 19–20, 38, 42
self-confidence, lack of 43, 139
self-esteem, low 47, 135
    and depression 19, 20
self-harm 31–4, 122
self-help groups 79–80, 106
self-hypnosis 52
Selye, Hans 41
Serenace 125
Serenid-D 128
serotonin 20
sexual issues:
    and anorexia 12
    disinterest in 31
    fear of intercourse 10
    and Freudian analysis 68–9
    lack of inhibition 23
    relationship with therapist 82
    therapy on 79
shakiness 129
sharp objects, fear of 10
Shelter 89, 91
sheltered accommodation 89
sherry 58
shiatsu 143, 145
side-effects (of drugs) 125–9
Sinequan 127
single people, groups for 94
sleep:
    and exercise 61
    fear of 10
sleeping tablets 64, 65
sleeplessness 12, 30, 31, 43, 64–5
    and alternative treatments 138, 142
smoking 31, 43, 73, 133
social services departments 87
social workers, mental health 87, 98
social withdrawal 31, 43
sociopathic disorder 6, 34–5
soft drinks 59
Solis 129
Sommite 129
Sparine 125
spasms 126
special assessment and supervision
    service (SASS) unit 99–100
speech (*see also* talking):
    and disorder of expression 37
    fast 23
speed, fear of 10
spiders, fear of 10
spirits (alcohol) 58
'split personality' 35
stamina, building up 63

stared at, fear of being 9
starvation *see* anorexia; bulimia
Steiner, Rudolph 133
Stelazine 125
Stemetil 125
Stesolid 129
stomach pains 43
strangers, fear of 9
strength, building up 63
stress (*see also* tension) 7, 41–2
    and alternative therapies 134, 138,
        145
    causes of 44–7
    dealing with 48–55
    and drugs 126
    signs of 43–4
stress-management groups 93
stretching exercises 49–50, 63
strokes 18
sugar 59
suicide 31, 122
Sullivanian school 71
Sulpiridine 125
sun beds 31
supervised discharge 113
supervision orders 87
supervision registers 116
suppleness, building up 63
support groups 86, 92–3, 94
Surem 129
surgical operations 117
Surmontil 128
Survivors Speak Out 121–2
suspiciousness, feelings of 26
swimming 62, 63

tachophobia 10
T'ai chi 145
talking:
    constant 14
    importance of 54, 80
taphophobia 9
Taractan 125
tartrazine 60
tea 59
tearfulness 43, 49
telephone helplines 87, 94
Temazepam 129
tension 14, 31, 43
    dealing with 54–5, 138, 139
    and exercise 61
    and sleeplessness 65
thalassotherapy 142
thanatophobia 9

therapeutic communities 35, 99
therapies 66–7
    choosing 67–79
    monitoring progress in 82
therapists:
    choosing 80–1
    complaints against 82–3
    National Health Service 83
    private 81, 83–4
Thiopropazate 125
thought(s):
    disorder of 37
    repetitive 25
    see also mind control
thunder, fear of 10
tiredness 28, 42, 43, 133
tocophobia 9
Tofranil 127
torticollis 126
'touch for health' 134
tranquillisers 15, 23
    dependency on 22
    major 125–6
    minor 128–9
transference (of feelings) 69, 72, 82
Tranx 22
Tranxene 129
Tranylcypromine 128
travel, fear of 10
Trazodone 127
treatments:
    alternative 132–46
    drug *see* drug treatment
    ECT 22, 25, 227, 228, 130–1
    refusal of 104, 117–19, 124
treats 20, 64
tremor 127
Triazolam 128
tricyclic anti-depressants 127–8
Trifluoroperazine 125
Trifluperidon 125
Trimipramine 128
Triperidol 125
Tryptizol 127
twitches, nervous 43, 126

'unconscious, collective' 71

unemployment benefit 88
unhappiness 5, 21
Unisomnia 129
United Kingdom Council for
    Psychotherapy (UKCP) 81, 83
university counselling courses 84
urinary problems 127, 129

Valium 129
Valrelease 129
vegetables 60, 61
venereal disease, fear of
    (venerophobia) 10
Vertigon spansules 125
Vietnam veterans 40
Viloxazine 128
vision, blurred 127
Vivalan 128
voices, hearing 4, 5, 36
voluntary counselling agencies 83
voluntary organisations 93–4
Voluntary Services Group 65

ward rounds, hospital 100–2
water 61
    fear of 10
    see also hydrotherapy
Watts, Geoff 141
weight loss, obsession with *see*
    anorexia
weight-training 62, 63
Westminster Pastoral Foundation 83
wine 58
'winter blues' 30–1
women, fear of 10
words, disordered 37
work 55, *see also* overwork
worms, fear of 10
wounding oneself 31, 32, 34

Xanax 128
xenophobia 9

YMCAs 89, 91
yoga 53–4, 145–6

zoophobia 9